LOOK AT ME,
LOOK
AT
ME!

LOOK AT ME, LOOK AT ME!

DOM JOLY

BLOOMSBURY

First published in Great Britain 2004
This paperback edition published 2005

The author assures the publishers that everything in this book is
completely true – as far as he remembers, given that he has been quite
heavily medicated for several prolonged periods of his life, and has a
crippling substance abuse condition that has led to frequent blackouts,
and almost non-existent long-term memory. He has, therefore,
subsequently pointed out that, although to the best of his knowledge
this is an accurate summation of his life, it might be total bollocks.
He's frankly not sure. Hope this is of help while reading the following.

Plate section design by Katie Tooke

Bloomsbury Publishing Plc, 36 Soho Square, London W1D 3QY

A CIP catalogue record for this book is available from the British
Library

ISBN 0 7475 7760 9
9780747577607

10 9 8 7 6 5 4 3 2 1

All papers used by Bloomsbury Publishing are natural,
recyclable products made from wood grown in well-managed forests.
The manufacturing processes conform to the
environmental regulations of the country of origin.

Typeset by Palimpsest Book Production Limited, Polmont, Stirlingshire

Printed in Great Britain by Clays Ltd, St Ives plc

www.bloomsbury.com/domjoly

To my gorgeous wife, Stacey, and my lovely little Parker and Jackson. Thank you so much for supporting me and enabling me to do all the things I do.
I love you all very, very much.

"Look at me!
Look at me!
Look at me NOW!
It is fun to have fun
But you have to know how.
I can hold up the cup
And the milk and the cake!
I can hold up these books!
And the fish on a rake!
I can hold the toy ship
And a little toy man!
And look! With my tail
I can hold a red fan!
I can fan with the fan
As I hop on the ball!
But that is not all.
Oh, no.
That is not all...."

That is what the cat said...
Then he fell on his head!

From *The Cat in the Hat*
by Dr. Seuss

CONTENTS

Little Me

MY BIRTH WAS very different from what I'd expected. I'd always envisaged something moody – low lights and a cool tune hovering around in the ether, maybe something by Jacques Brel? Things rarely go to plan.

I was torpedoed into a dimly lit room where my mother was hooked up to some very low-fi equipment and surrounded by several tired-looking men in ill-fitting moustaches. There was a cool second of calm as we all looked at each other in a slightly disappointed manner before I was grabbed by an aggressive-looking fat woman, flung into a sink and sprayed with cold, slightly muddy-looking water.

I think that I was an unusual baby. I had a full, thick head of hair and a complete set of teeth – not that common in a newborn. I lay there, soaking wet and a bit depressed. Then I heard the hissy tones of a tinny wireless in the corner of the room. I strained to recognise the tune . . . it was 'House of the Rising Sun' by The Animals. Fucking hell! I was a Sixties child. I was going to have to cope with all the hippy dippy flower power, peace man crap that came with it. I didn't want to. I tried to crawl back towards the safety of the womb, but it was too late.

And that wasn't all. As I took a better look around the room it became very clear that this wasn't England. As they wheeled me into some sort of ward I tried to work it out.

Blue-robed men ran around screaming and stabbing patients with dangerous-looking syringes and veiled women occasionally came up to my cot, grabbed my cheeks and made weird nasal noises of delight. If I could have run I would have done, but I was trapped, trapped in a mind that wanted out with a body that couldn't deal with bladder control never mind a getaway car.

From fleeting snatches of conversation I gathered that I was in a hospital somewhere in the Middle East. The nurse's conversation flittered between Arabic, French and English. Where the hell was I? It sounded like the rehearsal rooms for *Mind Your Language*. A portly-looking woman leaned over my cot and made another grab for my cheeks. Enough was enough. I decided that if I was in the Middle East then I needed to draw my first line in the sand. As her overly glossed lips hovered over my face I took the initiative and sank my impressive virgin teeth into her stubbly olive chin. To my three-hours-old self, the scream was like nothing I'd ever heard. To this day, I still rate it as a top ten.

My parents took me away from the hospital very soon after. As I lay in the back of their car, homeward bound, I began to take in my surroundings: Mediterranean climate, exotic-looking population, anarchic mix of architecture – and guns, lots of guns. 'Welcome to Lebanon' screamed a large sign by the side of the airport road. Well, it wasn't England, but it could have been worse – it could have been Vietnam. I decided to get some sleep. It had been a long day. I dozed off, twenty-seven hours old, racing towards a new home and a new life. Home was a large house in the hills above Beirut. My parents lived at the top of the house and my quarters were down in the basement in the nursery.

2

Living with me in the nursery was my nanny. A fearsome Armenian woman, it quickly became clear that she had no real truck with children. She didn't speak a word of English and made her wishes known through a series of clicks, grunts and hand waving. I soon got the hang of it all. She watched a lot of TV: Armenian TV, which is even worse than Italian. It seemed to consist of footage of a small room with a lot of chairs in it, like a large wake. A big fat man sat in the centre of the room and about a dozen other men sat around him. They were all smoking and shouting and drinking coffee. Occasionally the programme would break away from the wake and go to some am-dram production that was filmed by an am-sham cameraman who seemed to be sitting in the audience with the camera secreted in his robes. My nanny, Suleikissan, would sit glued to the goggle box for hours, quite forgetting that I was around. This allowed me to do what I liked in my little subterranean home. I learned to crawl very early, at about two months old. I think that I realised that it was an early priority. Our quarters consisted of two adjoining rooms: one for me and one for Suleikissan. We shared a small bathroom with a weird half-bath which you sat in like an armchair. Our windows looked out onto the nursery garden where a Union Jack fluttered in the warm wind that came up the mountain off the sea far below. Down a dark corridor were two further bedrooms where the cook and the maid slept. At the far end was a sinister boiler room that made weird noises and belched smelly black smoke out of a small window. Suleikissan was terrified of it and thought that some monster lived in there. I was fairly sure that it was me that was supposed to think that and have her comfort me. Things didn't really work that way. I was fascinated by it and it didn't take me long to work out how to open the door and explore. It was in there that I met Arthur, a large Rhodesian Ridgeback who liked to sleep in there because it was warm and no one bothered him. Arthur was not what you might call a people person. At first I didn't notice him as he was a gorgeous rusty brown and blended well into the shadows. 'What the fuck are you doing in here?' he growled. I was relatively unfazed by a talking dog. After all he was the first one I'd met apart from Scooby Doo and he was dubbed in to only spoke Armenian. 'Hello,' I replied. 'Who are you?' The Ridgeback raised himself lazily to his feet and stretched his limbs in a slightly poncey manner.

'I'm Arthur, I've been wondering when we'd have a chat. I've been going fucking crazy with all your wailing and shouting.'

'That wasn't me,' I replied quickly. 'That must have been Armenian telly, they're always shouting about something. I can't understand a word of it.' The dog looked thoughtful for a moment and then extended an elegant, languid paw.

'I'm Arthur,' he said. 'Looks like we'll be seeing a lot of each other whether I fucking like it or not, so we'd better get to know each other.' I had never really heard anyone swear before. Suleikissan used to get angry and shout stuff at her sister on the phone but it was in Armenian so I never really picked it up. I liked Arthur. He was quite cool. He picked me up by the nappy and took me on a little tour of the house. He padded upstairs and showed me the kitchen, the large dining room, the drawing room and the study. A large balcony wrapped itself around the front of the house with wonderful views down to Beirut and the Mediterranean.

'You've lucked out here,' said Arthur. 'They're a nice family

4

and the location is spot on. You'll like it.' He picked me up again and took me upstairs to the top floor. There were five bedrooms, a couple of bathrooms and another wraparound balcony with even better views of the Lebanese capital.

'Come and see the garden,' said Arthur. But before he could pick me up my mother stormed in.

'What on earth are you doing up here?' she shouted. I turned to Arthur assuming that he'd explain that he was giving me the grand tour. He was already halfway downstairs. I smiled sweetly at my mother and tried to make an endearing baby sound but she thought I was going to be sick and wrapped me in a blanket. She picked me up and carried me down to the nursery.

When I bumped into Arthur the next day I asked him why he hadn't explained that it was him who'd brought me upstairs.

'I don't talk to adults, it all gets a bit too complicated. I just play the dumb dog and get my nosh off them.' I was secretly pleased that he talked to me but opted to hide my pleasure from my four-legged friend. The next couple of months were a bit difficult. Clearly, Suleikissan had been given a bit of a bollocking by my mother. She watched a little less telly and spent more time grunting at me. However, the lure of Armenian primetime soon wore her down and I managed to start meeting up with Arthur again. We would sit in the boiler room and he filled me in on a bit of family history. Arthur knew a great deal about the family, probably more than anyone as he was an obsessive eavesdropper and no one worried about what they said in front of a dog. He leaned back on the pile of old cushions that he had amassed over the years and began his story.

My great-grandfather was English and lived in London in the Victorian era. He was what Arthur called 'a bit of a chancer'. He worked in a small company in Holborn that made homeopathic medicine for very rich women with little else to do but become pathological hypochondriacs. Great-grandpa was a bit of a charmer and quite a hit with some of these ladies. He had absolutely no training in homeopathy but, seeing the whole thing take off, he decided to set up his own business just off Marylebone High Street.

Joly Fyne Homeopathic Remedys (sic) was born and great-grandpa brought his old clients with him and did a roaring trade. He noticed that the more exotic the remedy, the more thrilled the ladies. They loved the obscure names that he gave his potions. There were things like 'Mr Joly's Rabbit's Bottom Powder' (for self-doubt and melancholy). Then there was 'Mr Joly's Lady's Relish' (to be eaten on bread and supposed to cure constipation immediately). As more and more ladies flocked to his door, 'and to his bed,' added Arthur with a lascivious wink, he struggled to keep the ladies' interest and come up with more inventive potions and lotions. Then one week he appeared to make a breakthrough. He unveiled a whole new range of elixirs ranging from 'Mr Joly's Tapir Tapenade' (on bread for tuberculosis) to 'Mr Joly's Pygmy Hippopotamus Toe-powder' (for piles). He told anyone who cared to ask that he had gone into business with a slave trader from Bristol, who, now slavery had been abolished, was looking to get into other fields.

He would sail the seven seas bringing Mr Joly back the exotic species that were needed for his burgeoning business. The new elixirs were an enormous hit and Mr Joly even made it onto the cover of the *London Illustrated News* as part of their 'London's Most Esteemed Establishments Special Edition'. Great-grandpa was fast becoming a very rich man. He bought a house in Mayfair and a car with a top speed of twelve miles an hour. He was the first person in London to do away with a man preceding his vehicle with a red flag and became known, rather weakly, as 'Mr Joly Speedy' in society gossip columns. It was not to last.

For several months the London papers had been full of stories about the rapidly disappearing population of the new zoo in Regent's Park. Keepers would find their cages empty in the morning and experts were brought in to speculate about what might have happened to them. Some thought that the beasts had simply shrivelled up and died because of the English weather. Others blamed a small population of Ceylonese living in St John's Wood who were rumoured to eat all sorts of things. They were burned out of their houses by a dim mob who, encouraged by their success, marched down to South Kensington and burned down the original Natural History Museum because someone had seen bones in there. The mob was finally broken up by the infamous Bow Street Clobbers. They clubbed two men to death before the crowd dispersed.

'They needed a couple of fucking Ridgebacks, that would have sorted the fuckers out,' said Arthur menacingly. I nodded my approval, thinking how handsome Arthur looked when he was angry.

The game was eventually up when my great-grandpa was caught climbing out of the penguin pond clutching a bag containing four chloroformed penguins. He tried to pass it off as a drunken prank until one of the policemen recognised him from the article in the *London Illustrated News*.

By the next day, the story was all over town and when the police searched his office and the house in Mayfair they discovered sacks and sacks of dismembered animals, birds and reptiles, as well as an extraordinary collection of pornographic slides of pygmies in erotic poses. He fled the country the next day along with his clearly mortified wife, a rather tall woman. There is still a plaque on a wall opposite the new penguin enclosure marking the site where my great-grandfather was arrested with his bag of unconscious penguins.

'They fuck you up, your great-grandmum and dad,' laughed Arthur. I smiled at him uneasily, not getting the reference. Arthur was surprisingly well read. I'd had enough family history for the day so we went out into the garden and Arthur helped me dig a couple of big holes in the lower garden which we covered with bamboo and leaves. It was one of our favourite pastimes and we had got three gardeners so far. One of them had been stuck overnight until my mother heard his screams. So that was that. The months slipped by and I was very happy in my basement and with my little existence. Arthur taught me a lot in those early months. There was a slight hiccup when I inadvertently killed Suleikissan but it wasn't really my fault. She was having one of her rare baths and was singing some Armenian folk tune at the top of her tone-deaf voice. She used to drag her bedside lamp into the little bathroom so that she could read an appalling magazine called *Monday Morning*. It was the Beirut precursor to *Hello* magazine but, without the advantage of any stars or personalities, was merely a series of crap photos of overly made-up women at cocktail parties talking to fat middle-aged men smoking cigars. It was more like a newsletter from some middle-ranking bank than a society magazine. Suleikissan loved it.

Anyway, I heard her in the bath and thought that I would surprise her by bursting in. I loved doing this as she normally dropped *Monday Morning* into the bath and then tried to chase me down the corridor, dripping wet. I hit the door slightly harder than normal and it flew open, catching the gilt edge of the lamp that was perched precariously on top of the cistern. The lamp toppled in slow motion into the bath and there was a small bang, a flash of blue light and a slight sizzling sound. Suleikissan went rigid, her pendulous breasts pert for the first (and last) time in over forty years. She went bright red then blue then black and slumped backwards against the wall. Her copy of *Monday Morning* floated upside down in the water. I can still remember the headline: 'Bulgarian trade delegation guests of honour at Ministry of Trade's cocktail party'. I didn't really realise what I'd done until Arthur came in and explained it to me. His advice was to bugger off and let someone else discover it. 'Maybe they'll blame that fucking cat,' he grinned. He hated the family cat and never missed a chance to give it hell. We wandered off into the garden to check our man-traps and almost forgot about the whole thing until we heard screams from the house.

Once Upon a Time in Beirut

I THINK THAT MY parents felt a bit guilty about the whole
nanny-killing incident as I started to see a lot more of
them than I had previously. They employed another woman
called Sylvia who was English but she only looked after me
in the evenings. I spent most of the days upstairs with my
mother, my brother and my sister whose existence I had
been unaware of until Suleikissan's passing. My mother was
a quiet woman who had a terrible speech impediment that
made her very introverted. She didn't really seem to know
what to do with me so I was expected to entertain myself.
I would spend hours waiting for the phone to ring so that
I could listen to her attempt to answer it. By the time she
finally got the word 'hello' out, the caller had invariably
hung up. According to Arthur, she had got the stammer late
in life when she'd had to do some charity auction in Beirut.
She had been nominated as the auctioneer and had become
so nervous and worked up about it that, when the day
came, she was mute. When she recovered her speech she
had this terrible stammer that made it very difficult for her
to communicate. And the phone made it ten times worse.

My brother and sister were about ten years older than
me and not too keen on my recent appearance. When I
think of them, I think of potatoes. They both had spud-
guns, a type of gun that you loaded by sticking the muzzle

into a potato. It fired rotten, mushy bits of potato at quite some velocity and I was on the receiving end most days. In fact for quite a long period of my youth I constantly smelled of old potato. This gave me a profound allergy to the potato that has stayed with me ever since. Any contact with one brings me out in a hideous rash. My brother was of Chinese origin and this was never clearly explained. Not even Arthur was completely sure how this had happened. Apparently my dad had spent a 'lost weekend' in Shanghai some time back and my brother had arrived some time after that but that was all that was known. His English was not brilliant, so communication was also fairly minimal. My sister was more communicative although, sadly, a dwarf. It was apparently a hereditary condition in the family.

To avoid the potato assaults, I used to spend time in the potting shed in the garden. It was a good hiding place and I could get a bit of peace and quiet in there. Arthur knew that I went in there and he would come and visit me.

I told him that I was not really enjoying living upstairs. He told me that things would get better as I got used to it. To pass the time Arthur told me stories about my family history. He loved an audience and would hold forth for many happy hours as we sat amongst the piles of compost, old terracotta pots and a selection of outgrown bicycles. My disgraced great-grandparents, I learned, slipped over the Channel to France but, as my great-grandfather thought the French more unhygienic than rats, they continued on to Switzerland. It seems that he fabricated a new past for them all and somehow got into making watches. He had no formal training but, true to character, this didn't seem to stop him. He used the trading name 'Jolytime' and produced a series of low-end watches that did quite well with people who'd never been able to afford one before. The very best model gained over an hour a day but fortunately these were the days before consumer checks and he managed to make a decent living. He died in 1910 and was buried in the village that he'd settled in. Arthur said he had seen pictures that my parents had of the gravestone. It read: 'Here lies Herbert Remus Joly. Englishman. Ruined it for everyone.' I don't think that my great-grandmother ever really forgave him. My grandfather was born nine months after they arrived in Switzerland.

'That was your great-grandfather trying to get her to forget about the fucking porn and the dwarves,' said Arthur.

'I thought that they were pygmies?' I said.

'All the same, aren't they? Fucking dwarves, pygmies. It doesn't matter whether your sister is a dwarf or an elf, does it? She's still a short-arse.' I nodded and Arthur continued.

My grandfather lived in Switzerland until he was sixteen. At school he learned of clocks, cuckoos and cheese. Swiss military history consisted of just one lesson. A rather sheepish man would tell them about an Italian army patrol that took a wrong turn and ended up on Swiss soil. The local Swiss policeman politely asked them what they thought they were doing. The Italians panicked and hotfooted it back the way they came. This was Switzerland's one and only military campaign and it held a special place in Swiss hearts. My grandfather was bored. Switzerland seemed to be a place where rich Europeans came to die peacefully, punctually and without any litter. Children were put up with but not encouraged. The main excitement was the weekly trip to the railway station to await the arrival of the train from

Geneva. As the train pulled in all the children would watch the station clock and nod approvingly as the second hand hit twelve o'clock the very second the train's brakes brought the locomotive to a full stop. Everyone cheered and clapped this remarkable show of Swiss efficiency. They would all check that their watches corresponded exactly with the station clock and then wander off down the hill to the village for some melted cheese. Everyone that is, except my grandfather, who wore a 'Jolytime' watch. It was always seven hours too fast and had to be adjusted. On his sixteenth birthday, my grandfather bade farewell to his parents, packed some cheese into a small rucksack and set off to see the world. He would never return. From what we know, he avoided France since he held the same views as his father and headed south into Italy. Extraordinarily he got a job in Siena as a jockey. My grandfather was a small man and the locals needed his type to take part in the annual race around the town square known as the 'Palio'.

For this event, the city was divided into ten different areas and each area had their own colours, traditions and fierce passion. There had long been a tradition of getting jockeys from afar so that there would be less danger of them being bribed. Traditionally the jockeys had been brought over from Sicily where a lot of the menfolk were short in stature. Sadly, the whole little-man syndrome had totally overtaken the island. Every village in Sicily was bursting with short, angry men, stripped to the waist and looking for an excuse to start a fight.

In a couple of years, these same aggressive little men would channel their anger into organised crime and start their invasion of the USA. For now the whole island was a nonstop fistfight and no one had the time to be jockeys any more. My grandfather had inherited the gift of the gab from his father and quickly convinced the Siennese that he was an experienced jockey, well known in the Swiss racing fraternity.

The Palio is like no other race in the world. On the day of the race, the entire town turns out for the spectacle, filling every available viewpoint. A rough track is prepared by laying sawdust around the edges of the square. To the newcomer it's a tableau straight out of the Middle Ages. Once the race is under way there are no real rules, beyond that the first horse and rider to complete the circuit eight times is the winner.

Although inexperienced, my grandfather was a natural horseman and got to grips with the whole thing fairly quickly. Come the day of the Palio, he apparently had appalling food poisoning from the banquet the night before. There was suspicion that he had been deliberately poisoned but there was no question of him not taking part.

'Probably a dodgy kebab the night before. That's the problem with fucking foreign food, no fucking idea of basic hygiene,' growled Arthur.

Photographs of my grandfather at the start of the race show a sallow, slightly perturbed young man, looking resplendent in the blue colours of his area. What could have been going through his young head as he prepared to take part in the most dangerous horse race in the world? In the past, losing jockeys had been torn apart by their own supporters for coming second. One unfortunate was spit-roasted and fed to his own horse. It was in this charged atmosphere that my grandfather geared up at the starting line.

'I presume that whatever happened it couldn't have been worse than living in fucking Switzerland,' chuckled Arthur.

The race was one of the tightest in years with all eight horses neck and neck. Jockey whipped jockey, spectators bayed for blood and my grandfather felt a little queasy. Suddenly he found himself on the inside of the group as they turned by the clock tower for the last time. He saw a small gap and his horse lunged forward into the lead. He screamed out loud with excitement and this was, unfortunately, the final straw for his delicate insides. A mixture of nerves, raw veal, adrenaline and vats of potent local wine all caused him to vomit like no man had ever vomited before (it was actually a criminal offence in Switzerland until 1984 punishable by six months in a very clean prison). A revolting, viscous carpet of sick covered the track behind him as his horse charged on. The pursuing horses stood no chance. Already knackered, they had nothing left to keep themselves standing. Seven horses and their riders went tumbling over in an unedifying pile of horse, vomit and rider. Three jockeys were killed and two spectators were crushed to death by a stand knocked over in the pile-up. My grandfather rode into victory and Siennese history as the Palio's first Swiss winner.

That night he was the king of the world. After he'd been cleaned up, he and the horse were carried through the streets of north east Siena and into a cathedral for a celebratory mass. Afterwards they were guests of honour at an enormous dinner held in the main street. He was given the pick of the local beauties to sit next to him that evening. The woman he chose, Cara, was to become my grandmother. To this day, on 18th July every year my whole family gather round a groaning dinner table and eat and drink until everyone at the table has vomited. It's a question of honour as well as an excuse to totally pig out.

'Fucking disgusting if you ask me,' said Arthur. 'I fuck off to one of my bitches' houses for a couple of days when that shit goes on, not my scene at all.'

But good luck was not always to follow my grandfather. In November 1914 he and Cara were on a holiday in Constantinople when the First World War broke out. As he still had a British passport and Cara was an Italian they were arrested by the Ottomans and, after a period of internment in Smyrna, were force marched with about two hundred other prisoners of war for over three weeks down into what is now Syria where, for the duration of the war, they were held captive in an old crusader castle.

Upon their release my grandfather ended up in a port town called Beirut on the coast of the French protectorate, Syria. They adored the country and, despite my grandfather's strongly held views on the French, decided to stay there. I think he felt that by being in there early enough he could help to shape future hygiene habits. And this became his *métier*. To the bafflement of the French inhabitants he and Cara set up a shop selling beauty and hygiene products whilst Cara used the big room at the back to give massages that she had learned to give in the crusader castle off a Hungarian inmate who used to work at the Gellert baths. She didn't do the whole beating with eucalyptus thing but it became very popular with locals.

So they settled in Lebanon and built a large house in the hills overlooking the future Lebanese capital. Soon they had a son, my father, and the family was complete. He grew up there but was sent to boarding school in England. Having gone to Cambridge University, he returned to Beirut intent on starting his own business. For reasons best known to himself he set up a company importing clown costumes for children's entertainers all over the Middle East. Arthur said that I would get a new clown's costume every Christmas and would be encouraged to dress up in them when potential clients came round to the house. I told Arthur it all sounded a little odd. He said it was fine, nothing to worry about.

Looking back now, I realise that this was all a subconscious beginning to what would eventually become my career. It has unfortunately left me with a severe case of coulrophobia, a terrible phobia of clowns and children's entertainers of any kind. But I am not alone in this. Some of the biggest names in the entertainment business suffer from it – P. Diddy, Alan Hansen, Jodie Marsh, to name but three. It doesn't usually have any great effect on my everyday life, though I once went to a friend's child's birthday party without realising that she'd booked a clown. When he entered the room I panicked, punching the poor fellow several times in the face before running out of the house screaming. The charges were eventually dropped and my friends all now know not to book clowns when I'm around.

My dad's business went from strength to strength. He even developed a fundamentalist clown costume for the more religious areas of the Arab world. This meant that the entertainer had to make an enormous use of their eyelids and lashes to be successful as the costume hid everything else.

My mother was brought up in Somerset where her family

had lived for generations. They made lawnmowers and patented the very first sit-on model. Unfortunately they didn't think of including an engine; theirs was a pedal-powered one. Although feasibly it could have done very well in today's more fitness obsessed market, back then it proved to be a non-seller. The company went bust when my mother was fourteen and she was pulled out of school and sent to work immediately to keep the family going. She became one of the first women apprentice butchers in Somerset. By the age of eighteen she could dissect an entire cow in under an hour but this wasn't enough for her. She wanted to see the world. On her nineteenth birthday she flew the coop, hitch-hiked to Portsmouth and paid for passage on the first ship to leave port. The ship took her to Beirut where she fell in love with a halal butcher. They had a torrid six-month affair but eventually broke up, blaming it on irreconcilable filleting differences. Two months later she met my father. They were an odd couple but seemed to have come to an arrangement over the years and both seemed perfectly content with their disjointed lives. They didn't see that much of each other since my father was often away travelling and my mother was very much a homebody. Arthur also told me what to expect in the future. 'When you get a bit older they'll send you to a place called school where you'll spend the first couple of years pouring paint on bits of paper which your parents will put up on the fridge for a couple of weeks until you bring home a new one.'

I asked Arthur whether he'd ever talked to any other humans.

'No, not really,' he replied.

'You're the first one that I've really got to know. I chat

to the cat occasionally but he's an ignorant bastard, thinks he knows everything, you know the kind, cocky little fucker.' I nodded sympathetically. Arthur really hated that cat and it was best to let him vent when he got onto the subject.

As Arthur had warned me I was eventually sent off to the Lycée Français in West Beirut. It was an enormous place made almost entirely out of bare concrete. It looked just like a prison which I soon realised was no coincidence. The uniform was a weird pale blue smock that made us all look like a troupe of rather camp artists. The real troubles in Lebanon hadn't kicked off by then and Beirut was still the destination for Moslems looking for a bit of a break from their stricter homelands. Up the coast from Beirut, the Casino Du Liban mixed gambling with dancing girls to the great delight of the many Saudi Arabians who visited. Beirut itself was chock-a-block full of great restaurants, nightclubs and just about anything else that money could buy. It was natural then that these visitors would also think of sending their kids here for a good French education. This gave them a cast-iron reason to visit on a regular basis. One of these children was to become my best friend at the Lycée. We met on my first day in maths class. His name was Uday and his dad was something big in Iraq. I warmed to him immediately. He seemed sensitive, a little shy and yet there was something steely about him that meant (in Arthur's words) 'that you didn't fuck with him'. Maybe it was the way that he carried a small, engraved switchblade or the calm assurance with which he smacked an older boy over the head with a stick when he jumped the queue at break. It was difficult to tell but I was lonely and I felt a strong affinity with him straight away. He was quite possessive and wasn't very keen on me making any other friends – in fact he got quite agitated if I so much as suggested that we play with anyone else.

The school was very strict and had a particularly strong code of discipline. If anyone misbehaved in class, then the teacher would send them to stand outside and wait for Monsieur Moulot. This was my first contact with true evil. A tall, thin, dark-haired man with small glasses and hairy hands, he looked like the sort of man who whipped cats for fun in his spare time. He would patrol the endless school corridors looking for unfortunates standing outside their classrooms. It was the waiting that got to you. He wore hard Cuban heels that made him seem even taller than he was. Long before you saw him you could hear the 'click, click' of his heels as he marched down a nearby corridor. When he saw you, a thin smile would appear on his face like that of a contented cheetah spying a wounded antelope. He toyed with you, slowing his walk and running the long metal ruler in his hands down the railings of the outside balcony. When he did reach you he would ask you why you were outside. It didn't really matter what you said. The punishment was always the same. Twelve hard blows to the outstretched palm of your left hand.

Uday would never show any emotion during these beatings. I would bawl like an English footballer but he would simply stare at Moulot, unblinking, unemotional. I used to wonder where this self-control came from. When I asked him he said that his dad beat him a lot and that if he cried out he would receive more. It was a control thing; he just switched off and that was that. I really admired him and felt that there was a lot that he wasn't telling me about his home life.

Uday and I used to spend a lot of time in the streets next to the school. There was a huge playground under the main class block where you were supposed to spend your breaks but it was a bit like a prison exercise yard with all sorts of dodgy shit going on. There were little fedayeen wannabees endlessly jumping over benches and rolling under fences. Pretend suicide bombers wandered around with bits of bamboo tied around their waists and mini Hezbollah kids would repeatedly whack themselves over the head with heavy school books until the blood poured down their angry little faces. It was a fucking nut house and Uday and I tried to keep well away.

The only time there was any sense of communal fun was when an Israeli jet roared over the capital on one of their many daily reconnaissance sorties over the city. As one, over a thousand kids would all form their hands into pistol shapes and make shooting noises at the jet. For about forty seconds the whole place united in its intensity of hatred directed at this tiny speck in the sky. Then the plane would disappear and everyone would get back to whatever role they were playing in this angry little world we were inmates in.

Uday and I would sit on the front steps of one of the sand-coloured apartment blocks opposite the school. We would watch the hundreds of street hawkers plying their illicit wares around the gates of the school. You could buy anything for the right price. Old men carried small boxes of plastic toys and Arab cartoon books whilst women would be selling freshly squeezed orange juice and small bags of nuts. Elsewhere, young street urchins laid out blankets covered with various car parts that they'd managed to steal from the car parks of the plush golf clubs and private beaches that bordered the shanty-towns and refugee camps. Lebanon was a cauldron of resentment and hatred just waiting to explode.

One morning Uday and I had both been sent out of our English lesson for passing each other notes. When Moulot found us, it was clear he had it in for Uday, as he started shouting at him in Arabic and slapping him across the face. I made out the words 'son of a dog' in my broken Arabic before Uday snapped. He pulled the switchblade out of his pocket and slashed it across Moulot's outstretched hand. Moulot turned white as a sheet, his mouth hanging open in disbelief as he stared at his injured hand, pumping out blood like a water sprinkler. He crumpled to the ground, pleading for help. I retreated towards the classroom door in total panic. Uday calmly put the knife away, aimed a kick at Moulot's face and walked off with a serene look on his little face. It was to be our last day at the Lycée.

We were moved to separate schools after that. My parents were clearly horrified and made sure that we did not keep in contact. I went to an American Quaker school up in the hills above Beirut nearer to home. I often wonder what happened to my little friend. He had clearly had a hard time at home and found it difficult to cope with life. I hope that he sorted himself out and made a success of himself. I expect that he became a doctor or something. It would be great if one day our paths crossed again.

The situation in Lebanon had got a lot worse by the time I started at my new school and my parents were actually quite relieved that I wasn't in Beirut. The beginnings of the civil war that was to rip the country apart were well under way. There was talk of kidnappings and roadside executions and armed men wandered around our villages more and more brazenly. To me this was all very exciting and my friends and I started collecting and swapping bits of shrapnel and other military debris, bullets instead of marbles. I had a little suitcase that I kept my prize pieces in and I never went anywhere without it. Looking back, I suppose it was quite an unusual childhood. One day someone in my class brought in a severed human head in a plastic bag to show everyone. Three people had been executed in a quarry just below his house and he had snuck in afterwards and grabbed this horrific souvenir. I can still picture the frozen look of terror on the poor man's face. When I told my parents, it was the last straw. Two days later they told me that I was to go to school in England. I nodded but didn't have a clue what they were on about. I asked Arthur later and he looked sadder than I'd ever seen him.

'I've just got one piece of advice for you,' he whispered. 'Keep your mouth shut and your back to the wall.' Once again I was completely baffled. Apparently he'd once had an unwelcome experience with an overly attentive British bulldog. Two weeks later I was on a plane bound for England.

Such, Such Were the Joys

I WASN'T ACTUALLY told that I was going to boarding school. My parents claim that they simply forgot to tell me. It didn't make much difference anyway as it would have been impossible to conceive of what awaited me.

I remember flying to the UK. I had flown before to see relatives as an Unaccompanied Minor. Nowadays, everyone is aware of the problems of child abuse and vulnerable children but back then it seems that it was quite all right to publicise the fact. I would turn up at airports dressed like Little Lord Fauntleroy with a large sign saying 'Unaccompanied Minor' strung around my neck with my passport attached to it. It wouldn't be long before some elderly gentleman would accost you and ask you whether you'd be interested in coming to see his puppy. The funny thing was that these men always seemed to keep them in the loos. Suffice to say that I saw a lot of the world but never any puppies. When I flew with my parents they would always wonder why I insisted on going to every airport loo to 'have a look at the puppies'. You live and learn. It was a bit like the time, much later in life, when I was discussing having your temperature taken and at what stage did doctors stop putting the thermometer up your bum and start doing the under tongue method? From the stunned silence around me I quickly realised that I had been the only recipient of this peculiarly French medical practice. It left

25

me wondering whether I'd been secretly sexually abused for some years without even realising it. As I said, you live and learn.

Anyway my parents accompanied me to England this time. We had a couple of days in London that I quite enjoyed. We went to see the monkeys masturbate at London Zoo and had a look at the plaque celebrating my great-grandfather's achievements. I was strangely proud and had my picture taken by it, much to my dad's chagrin. We had a bit of a treat in that they were shooting an elephant that day. It had fallen into a ditch and couldn't get up again. They would normally have picked it up with a crane or something but apparently everyone was on strike and there wasn't anyone to do it. They shot him four times with some sort of starter's pistol before dragging him off presumably to be hacked up and served as elephant burgers in the canteen. The next day we got up very early and stood in a queue in Marylebone for over six hours. My parents said that this was a British tradition and that we were going to see something very special, a whole lot of wax models of famous people. This was my first and last visit to Madame Tussauds (who should, at the very least, be forced to be called Mrs Tussaud if she is going to work in England.) I wonder what happened to Monsieur Tussaud. Maybe he didn't approve of his wife's unhealthy obsession with making wax lookalike effigies of famous people and ended up in the boiling tub of wax himself. I have to say that it was the dullest experience imaginable and I still, to this day, try to shout a warning to unwitting tourists in the queue as I roar past them on my way to work.

The following day we drove out of London for a couple of hours before arriving in a rather neat and tidy little English town. We parked the car and entered a rather shabby-looking house and had tea with the owners. I remember thinking that they seemed to have an extraordinary amount of children for their age. I counted at least thirty running around screaming and crying. Then my parents left, bidding me farewell. I assumed that they were off shopping but my mother mentioned something about seeing me in a couple of months and what fun I'd have here. I was rather taken aback. If I was going to be given up for adoption then there were surely more needy couples than these two who seemed to have been procreating at a biblical rate. I watched my parents drive off down the road and realised that this was very much a new chapter in my little life. I had been condemned to five years without hope of parole in an English Penal Establishment or, as it was generally known, a prep school.

The first night was horrific. I was not the only one in this life-altering situation and many just couldn't cope. I was in a dormitory with eight other new arrivals and it was not a happy place. In the bed next to mine a small boy wept for two hours calling out for 'mumsy' before packing up his meagre belongings and making a run for it. He didn't get far. He was brought back into the dormitory by the housemaster and 'slippered' in front of all of us. We were soon to learn that a 'stiff upper lip' was what was required to get by in this institution. I would rather have had a 'leather arse' as this would have been infinitely more practical but didn't mention it as this would have simply brought me the same fate. I thought that I might break the ice and bond with my new friends by getting everyone together to have a look at my shrapnel collection. I proudly snapped open the clasps of my little black suitcase and laid out some of my finer pieces on the bed. It had the required effect. The whole dorm gazed on in wonder as I lifted up a prized piece of a 'Grad' missile with some Russian writing still visible on it. I was just passing round my assortment of anti-aircraft bullets when two of the boys got up and left the room. I thought they must simply be jealous and carried on passing some of the items around the remaining boys. Suddenly the dormitory door flew open and there was my housemaster and the two 'sneaks'. He moved very carefully towards my bed and asked everyone to leave the room quietly and without making any sudden moves. I tried to explain that there was absolutely no problem and that I'd bashed these things around all over the place without ever having an accident (apart from the incident with the old man and the grenade that we set up as a tripwire but we had no idea that it was active and hadn't meant to harm anyone. Anyway no one ever found out about it until now and if anyone's reading who knows him then I'm really sorry. It was just a joke, well to us anyway, probably less so to him and I recognise that.) We were all evacuated from the building and taken to another house for the night. I heard that at first the metalwork master was sent in to deal with my stuff. I don't think that he was in any way qualified for this. He had been something dodgy in Aden and had left under a cloud, something to do with interrogation and stuff. He was known as 'Electrode' by everyone at school. We never found out why, but there were loads of stories. Apparently one night he had some sort of flashback and was found by matron the next morning lashed naked to the First Fifteen rugby posts. It was supposed to be hushed up but the local paper got hold of it and we were all banned from buying it, which of course made us all rush out and get one.

Anyway, he apparently got very agitated when he saw the stuff laid out on my bed. He wanted to take it all away and chuck it into the river but the headmaster insisted he call the police. Electrode got all furtive and nervous when the police were mentioned and said that there was nothing to worry about, that all the stuff was harmless and that he would take it away. Two days later he appeared in metal class with an appalling burn all the way up his left cheek: no one said anything about it; it was that sort of place.

I was slippered in front of the whole house and it became quickly apparent to me that marbles, not military detritus, was the currency of the playground in this particular establishment. Although I was obviously devastated at the loss of my prized collection, the whole incident did serve to give me something of a reputation amongst my fellow inmates. I was henceforth known as 'Psycho' by everyone and given a pretty wide berth. This suited me fine and I played up to this reputation. I got a subscription to *Guns and Ammo* magazine and used to stick pictures of women in swimsuits wielding machine guns above my bed. It seemed to work as people often used to whisper about me when I was sitting near them. Someone wrote 'Joly is a twat' in the science block loos so I had clearly made a mark.

The school seemed to be geared towards producing people totally unprepared for the late-twentieth century. If the year had been 1877 then we would have been progressing very nicely. As it was I always had a terrible sense of being completely at odds with the vast majority of the outside world. The only contact that we ever had with it merely served to confirm that something was seriously wrong. We were allowed into town once a week to wander around aimlessly. It was called 'town hour' and I'm still not very sure what it was that we were supposed to do there. We weren't allowed any money so we just stuck our noses up against shop windows and tried to sneak into WH Smith's and peek at porn mags. That is, if we were fortunate enough to make it to the town centre. Gangs of local 'casuals' would almost always be at the end of the road waiting for us, resplendent in their bright-yellow Pringle jumpers and spotty foreheads covered by a foppish fringe of badly high-lighted hair. They looked like the recent victims of a partic-ularly nasty attack by a gang of pigeons. They would chase us and when we were caught we would get a good kicking. I don't know what it was that they disliked about us, maybe it was the school uniform?

It was an odd look to say the least. Think of those magnifi-cent pictures of the last Tsar of Russia and his family. Their youngest son was a haemophiliac and, therefore, quite a sensitive chap. For some reason his mother seemed very keen to emphasise this side of his nature and would dress him up in a mini sailor suit. The person who designed our school uniform was either very keen on Russian history, or a cunt. We sported baggy pantaloons, a frilly white shirt with ruffs that would make Laurence Llewelyn-Bowen shudder, a tight-fitting navy-blue blazer with brass buttons, all finished off with a white hat that made grown men cry with laughter. The only exception to this fancy dress was if the temperature rose above forty degrees centigrade for three consecutive days. Then we were allowed to wear shorts:

tight, tight shorts. This might have seemed acceptable if your dad was the Tsar and the date was 1911 but this was 1977 and so we were seriously fucked. A passer-by coming across the gang of spotty casuals giving us a good going over might have been forgiven for wondering whether he had unwittingly stepped onto the set of *A Clockwork Orange.*

Life was shit. What I never understood was that we were constantly being told that we were the lucky ones, the future establishment, masters of all we surveyed. To me it simply explained where the Tory party recruited its membership from. Our families had made or stolen the money to send us to this place and we were supposed to get a head start in life. What we actually got was a good kick in the head and the first gentle stirrings of agoraphobia.

The school had many traditions that it upheld with particular pride. One of these was the somewhat spartan practice of an early-morning swim for the whole school. For no particular reason we all had to be nude. Every morning, come rain or snow, I shared a swimming pool with four hundred or so other nude little boys. At the time I thought nothing of it. I just assumed that, like the thermometer up the bum, this was normal. I assume that there must have been a reason for it all, although I never actually discovered one. There were also school dances. Not the disco, like anywhere else. We were supposed to learn to waltz and to foxtrot and do an eightsome reel. No one ever explained why. I presume it was just assumed that we would all grow up and be invited to hunt balls and weddings in Scottish castles *à la* Richard Curtis where we could display our fancy footwork like some Victorian Travolta. As we didn't actually have any girls we were allowed one dance at the end of the Christmas term where girls from the nearby ladies' college were shipped in for an evening of archaic revelry. We practised hard all term for this momentous event. The problem was that we had to practise with other boys and so fifty per cent of us learned to dance like girls and were totally unable to take on the male role if we ever actually got to grips with a real girl. The other problem was that the 'girls' were all five years older than us and had absolutely no interest in having their toes trodden on by sweaty little pre-pubescents. I can't say that I have yet been in a situation where I have needed my limited female ballroom dancing skills since I left school but one never knows.

Then there was the school film club. Every Sunday we would all gather in the school hall where we would watch a film, chosen for us by the club. I never found out who was in the club but they clearly had a very specific world-view. Week after week the enormous reels of film would arrive in the projection gallery and we would all sit down to watch something like *The Guns of Navarone* or *Where Eagles Dare* or *The Bridge Over the River Kwai*. I began to suspect that whoever did choose these films was quite a lot older than us and had never really got over the Second World War. Whoever it was, they definitely clouded our world-view and made life very difficult for the odd German or Japanese boy who had the misfortune to have been sent there. To us the world was full of either decent, brave Englishmen or nasty, cruel 'Nips' and 'Krauts'. A lot of my fellow inmates are now at a certain level in the Conservative Party and seem to be still watching the same films.

Meanwhile out in the real world, punk had exploded

onto the scene and we gleamed tantalising titbits from vehemently disapproving articles in the *Daily Mail*, the newspaper of choice. Someone smuggled in a tape of the Sex Pistols' *Never Mind the Bollocks*, oozing with illicit excitement and danger. It was such a sharp contrast to our daily diet of Latin and Gilbert and Sullivan that it made me feel quite giddy with excitement for the real world. Sadly it was to be some time until I was released into it. My holidays in Lebanon were as detached from reality as my Victorian schooldays.

The country had descended into a hideous civil war and was in meltdown. Almost all of my Lebanese friends were already in some way involved in the conflict. Some simply made up the equivalent of a junior dad's army, ready to defend their neighbourhood should the need arise whilst their fathers were off at the various flashpoints of proper conflict. Others were fully signed-up members of the militias fighting on the streets, using weapons almost too heavy for them to carry. It all came too easy. I started hanging out with a couple of them and before I knew it I was a member of a Phalangist militia outfit, swaggering around with an old Czech machine gun. I would tell my parents that I was off to a friend's house and we would all pile into his elder brother's jeep and roar off down to the so-called 'Green Line', the overgrown stretch of no-man's-land that separated Christian East Beirut from the Moslem West. There weren't really any rules. You just knew that the enemy were thataway and you hid behind sandbags and fired off clip after clip in their vague direction. I don't think that I ever saw any of them and, luckily, they didn't see me as I was never hit. The adrenaline rushes were extraordinary. I felt invincible, my gun slung awkwardly around my tiny shoulders, running from building to building shouting nonsense and trying to strike heroic poses in front of your friends. It was heady stuff. One day we were scouting around the old Beirut racecourse that was slap on the Green Line just behind the old museum that was now used as a sniper position by the Phalangists.

I was with Skander and Elias. Skander was older than Elias and I. He liked to think of himself as a bit of a veteran. He wore the obligatory outfit of a Beirut street fighter: long curly hair tied back with a bandana, tired blue jeans and an unbuttoned green khaki shirt that exposed his mass of chest hair to the world. He carried a pistol slung low on his hips in a holster, like he'd seen in cowboy films. Clipped to his belt were three pineapple-shaped grenades and he carried an AK47 Kalashnikov with two ammo clips taped to each other facing the opposite ways for a quick change. The AK47 was the machine gun of choice in Beirut as it had very few parts and rarely broke down. Elias and I looked slightly less cool. I was wearing a Pink Floyd T-shirt and some green cords that my mum had forced me to wear along with a really naff pair of brown sandals that she thought I looked 'sweet' in.

We were following Skander stealthily across the open ground of the racecourse heading for the deserted west stand from where we would have a good view over an area of West Beirut. As we neared the centre of the racecourse we heard someone shout and we legged it to the relative safety of the stand. We ducked down beneath it into a little tunnel that ran underneath the grandstand and stopped to catch our breath. We peered out through a grille and immediately saw where the shouting had come from. Across the dusty track we could see two angry-looking men coming in our direction. Skander and Elias didn't hesitate; they turned and ran as fast as they could down the tunnel. I went to follow them but the buckle from my bloody sandals broke and I fell, hitting my head on a handrail; everything went black.

When I came to, it took me a couple of seconds to focus. My head throbbed and when I touched it I could feel a damp patch on my forehead. I looked at my hand and it was covered in blood. I tried to move but something was holding my leg. A length of chain was clamped around my left leg and attached to a radiator. I looked around and saw that I was in a small room with no furniture. It was dimly lit from a tiny window in the top left-hand corner. I was sitting on a dirty blanket opposite a metal door that opened as I looked at it. Two men came into the room. One had a bottle of water and some form of meat wrapped in Arab bread on a smeggy plate. He put them down and left the room. The other man stood looking at me as the door shut behind the first one.

'What is your name?' he barked in Arabic.

'I don't speak Arabic,' I replied, trying to sound as English as possible.

'What is your name?' he repeated in pretty good English.

I desperately tried to think of what to do. My experience as a prisoner of war was mostly gleaned from the terrible films I'd seen at school and I knew that you were only supposed to give your name and number.

'My name is Dominic, number 2702,' I said, trying to sound relaxed.

'What is this 2702?' he bawled.

'It's my school locker number, I'm not really a soldier or anything, I was just playing around with some friends,' I whimpered.

'With a machine gun, what sort of game were you playing?' he snapped.

I tried to remember something from a film to help me out here but all I could think of was something like 'that's all you're getting from me, Fritz' or something about the Geneva Convention and none of this seemed particularly relevant. Prep school had left me singularly unprepared for anything like this, although living conditions were not that dissimilar.

'I want my mummy, let me go home,' I whined, sounding distinctly less relaxed.

He looked at me in complete disdain before turning on his heel and started to leave the room.

'You will be dealt with later,' he said as he slammed the door. I heard him laugh to himself as the thud of his footsteps evaporated down what sounded like a long corridor. I was starving and grabbed the sandwich and wolfed it down. It wasn't too bad, nothing worse than you'd get on the Edgware Road. I looked around my little cell and tried desperately to think about what to do. My parents wouldn't have a clue where I was and I had no idea whether Skander or Elias had even got away. Even if they had they wouldn't know what had happened to me. If this had happened a few years later then I would at least have had the opportunity to have heard stories of other Westerners in similar circumstances and I could have taken solace in the fact that things could have been a lot worse. After all, I could have been sharing my cell with Terry Waite who, if they gave

us a radio, would insist on hogging it and listening to the
religious programmes on the BBC World Service. He might
have insisted on trying to keep my spirits up by telling me
long, bad jokes. Then I'd have got his life story, over and
over again until I'd want to throttle him with his own
beard. No, I was in a pickle but, unbeknownst to me, I
could have been far worse off. I recalled watching *The Count
of Montecristo* and tried to remember what he'd done during
his long incarceration. All I could remember was that he'd
grown a long beard, made a rat his best friend and counted
the days by scratching them on the wall of his cell. Not
much bloody use to me – I wasn't even shaving so there
was no chance of getting a beard and I hated rats so that
was out of the question. I decided to start the wall diary
instead. I used the edge of the chain to make a small scratch
in the wall. There, that was my day's work done and it
had taken up about seven seconds. What now? I was going
to go mad. Maybe I already was mad? I started counting
the hairs on the back of my hand. Wasn't that the first sign
of madness? I didn't have any hairs on the back of my
hand or anywhere else really apart from on my head so
maybe I was OK? I remembered seeing *Papillon* and wished
that I hadn't fallen asleep halfway through. He definitely
escaped, something about swimming on a goatskin full of
air? Where the fuck was I going to find a goat and how
did you fill it with air? Anyway, I must be in Beirut so why
did I need to swim? I was definitely losing it. I suddenly
could see Arthur, clear as day. He was holding the cat by
its neck, throttling it, and repeating 'You're fucked' over
and over.

I fell asleep and had terrible dreams about the child-catcher in *Chitty Chitty Bang Bang*. Just as the child-catcher threw me into a well with a goat and I was slipping under the water, trying desperately to blow into the terrified creature's mouth, I woke up, soaking; I'd wet myself. This had been a recurring problem at school and one that had become quite a stigma. Bed-wetters were easy to spot as not only did we stink of urine but we were forced to have a plastic sheet fitted onto our mattresses. I was just coming to terms with this latest disaster when the door opened once again. It was the same man and he sniffed the air in disgust.

'Get up,' he commanded as he bent down, holding his nose, to unlock the chain that was still wrapped around my leg.

'Where am I going?' I asked, panicked.

'Shut up, follow me,' he said.

I got up and followed him down a dimly lit corridor. I tried desperately to keep calm but my mind was racing with the various possibilities that awaited me: a firing squad, a public stoning, maybe one of those drugged confessions that the Viet Cong used to get downed American pilots to read out before a quick kangaroo court and then a long slow death by having bamboo shoots grow through me. We went up some stairs and came into a sort of makeshift living room where the other man was sitting at a table drinking coffee. Out of the window I could see that I was still in the racecourse.

'Who are you?' I asked, as authoritatively as I could.

'You are tresspisser,' the first man said to me accusingly.

I could smell myself and had to admit that he wasn't far wrong but I was fairly sure that he wasn't talking about my little accident.

'You are tresspisser and if you come here again we call police,' said the man. 'We look after horses and all this bullshit, you no good here, fack off,' he continued, indicating an open door.

I tried to look confident as I edged towards the door suspecting some sort of trap. Surely they weren't going to let a dangerous street fighter like myself go? It had to be a trap.

'You fack off meester fack,' shouted the seated coffee drinker.

I didn't need any more encouragement and I sprinted out of the room, down some more stairs and out into an alley right next to the entrance that we had used to gain access in the first place. I ran as fast as I could towards the museum, expecting a volley of bullets to slam into my back at any moment. But none came. In the square opposite the museum I saw a Taxi Service, the communal taxis used all over the capital. I jumped in and threw all the money that I had in my pocket at the driver whilst shouting my address at him. He turned round slowly and gingerly picked up the piss-soaked notes and looked at me in bewilderment before turning round, pulling away from the square and heading towards the hills.

I got back home in time for supper and managed to change before my parents saw me. I made some terrible excuse about having fallen off a wall to account for the bruise on my head. My mother tut-tutted terribly and told me that I must be more careful. That night I crawled into bed and swore that, for me at least, the war was over.

It did make great material for my 'What I did in the holidays' essay when I got back to school, though it was very clear that no one believed me. I took a peek at some of the other essays and they were all about pony clubs, fishing in Scotland and one about a secret someone's uncle had sworn him to keep. This last one must have been pretty good because as soon as the teacher read it he was whisked off out of class and we never saw him again. His bags were packed by the time we got back to dorm. It was all right for some. I got a slippering and a long talk from my housemaster about how lying wasn't the best way to get on in life. I clearly had a good imagination, he said, so why not put it to good use and do some proper work? I gave up at that stage and never bothered to tell anyone about what used to happen to me in the holidays, since they obviously couldn't handle it. The story did get out though and my nickname changed from 'Psycho' to 'Lying Psycho' which wasn't very imaginative but stuck.

At thirteen things changed in all sorts of ways. I had to take Common Entrance in order to get into the public school of my parents' choice. I think the required pass rate was something around thirty per cent so I got a fairly good idea of how academic the school was going to be. I wasn't far wrong.

Another Country

PUBLIC SCHOOL WAS an extraordinary place. Mine was a minor one to the north of London and its principal purpose was to train people to run India. The advent of Indian independence shortly after the Second World War had put a fairly large stick in the school's spokes. It didn't seem to have ever found another purpose for itself so had pottered on minding its own business and hoping that no one would notice. It was what you'd expect from films, very *Another Country*. It had a large quadrangle, cloisters dominated by a large chapel and a rather different clientele from the old days. With Indian governance no longer on the agenda, the school had looked around for a new client base. These tended to be the newly wealthy children of nearby north London whose parents had been given a financial boost by Thatcher. Most of them were first-generation public-school boys and were still a bit rough round the edges. In truth, there was not a lot of difference between them and the gang of casuals that used to hang around my prep school waiting to give us a taste of their Sergio Tacchini slip-ons. The main problem that I faced, therefore, was not the random buggery and sadistic cruelty I had been led to expect, but, rather, that I was 'posh' and therefore needed taking down a peg or two. I was a little confused as I had been led to believe that the whole purpose of these establishments was to make us 'posh'. Britain was changing and so, it seemed, were its public schools.

There were various anachronisms that had survived the cull. We were forced to sleep in large, barn-like dormitories of fifty or so people. You started in a bed at the bottom of the barn and ended up, five years later, at the other end, progress of a sort, I suppose. The school had recently gone co-ed but only from the lower sixth upwards, so we were all boys until after O levels. This was particularly difficult as the changes I was going through were not purely social: puberty had raised its ugly head. A couple of weeks before I'd left my prep school all the leavers were taken into a room and given a special talk by the school doctor about 'things that we ought to know about'. There followed an excruciating talk about where things went and how babies were made, all illustrated by weird line drawings of men with beards and full-breasted women. It looked as though The Grateful Dead had commissioned an artist to come and sketch their backstage goings-on.

We collectively winced through the long, torturous hour it took for the doctor to tell us what was going to happen to us. Since the doctor was not married and had no children, we could only conclude that, like us, he found it all pretty revolting. The one thing that appeared vitally important was that our testicles dropped. This made everyone very nervous, so much so that people would suddenly announce to the dorm in the middle of the night that they were sure that it had happened. They would make an attempt to talk in a deeper voice for a while but they'd normally forgotten about it by supper time. I seem to remember having some sort of medical check when I arrived at public school and I'm fairly sure that the doctor did a 'testicle dropping' check but it might be my imagination. I can't remember having a positive visit to a doctor since the whole thermometer/bum incident so it's probably my fault but I tended to block out anything medical.

When I got home for the holidays my mother ttttttttttttttttttttold me that something had arrived from sssssssssssssschool and that it was on my bbbbbbbbbbbbbed and that I should ask her if there were any qqqqqqqqqqqquestions. I found a little booklet on my pillow called something like 'Questions Boys Often Ask.' To my horror it was a follow-on from the Grateful Dead sex talk and had more of the weird line drawings and a whole chapter on the 'testicle drop'. By this time I was absolutely petrified and sat, beetroot red, at the breakfast table the next morning praying that no one would ask me anything about it. In the end my mother simply asked whether I had any qqqqqqqquestions and I shook my head violently and looked deep into my cereal. I think she was as relieved as I was. I just wished everyone would leave my testicles alone.

I think that I first realised that 'it' had happened when I had to sit next to one of the sixth form girls in the school dining room. She was a gorgeous, sultry-looking blonde with magnificent breasts and huge bee-stung lips. She wasn't the brightest card in the pack but just looking at her it was very clear why she'd been allowed to come to our school. There were still enough heterosexual teachers to make the sensible decision.

On the day of my testicle drop she was talking to a friend of hers across the table. For some reason she had a copy of the first Men at Work album and they were both looking at the back sleeve. I was quietly eating my bowl of gruel when I suddenly started to get really hot and sweaty. I looked up and stared straight at the blonde. It was like someone had just switched on a light. Time stood still and the room started spinning. I could smell her Anaïs Anaïs and really wanted to touch her hair where it tumbled over her tight navy-blue jumper. My head filled with weird line drawings of breasts and a bearded man wearing small round glasses lying on a bed as the blonde sat astride him. 'Hop it, beardie, she's mine,' I heard myself saying out loud in a transitional high/low pitch. It came out rather too loudly and most of the table stopped talking. My bearded housemaster was particularly interested as he was in the middle of talking to a rather plain-looking girl next to him and he had obviously come to the conclusion that I was talking to him. He turned towards me and asked me whether there was any sort of problem. My hybrid high/low voice muttered a slightly squeaky denial before I went back to my gruel.

The blonde was in hysterics and her laughter had started shaking her breasts up and down in her tight jumper. I couldn't keep my eyes off her highly mobile nipples. I sat staring at them with a little bit of gruel dribbling down my face. Both she and her friend stopped laughing and stared at me in disgust as, with an utter lack of subtlety, I ogled her chest.

I can't remember whether it was a glass or a plate that hit me in the head but it really hurt and I felt blood pour down onto my forehead. The maelstrom that was raging in my head managed to calm itself for long enough to tell me to get out. I let out an ungodly scream that finally seemed to tear at my larynx and I suddenly became quite a deep baritone. As I ran out of the dining hall I realised between tears that 'it' had just happened: my voice had cracked and my testicles had dropped. I just hoped that this didn't spell more trouble. But I had underestimated the power of my new feelings for the blonde.

For the next month or so I became as close to a stalker as it was possible to be without being arrested. She made sure that she always sat as far away from me as possible. She would occasionally catch me staring at her and look away quickly. I would follow her at a distance when she was walking back to the girls' boarding house, ducking in and out of bushes to catch a glimpse of her. I cut out a picture of her from the school photo and kept it hidden in my desk, bringing it out now and then just to stare at it, unsure of what it was I was doing. I'd try to time my exit from my boarding house to coincide with hers. One day I managed it perfectly and I walked right behind her trying to look really casual whilst straining to get a glimpse of her legs as the material on her dress swish-swhished sexily in the wind. As I fixated on the thin slit of her skirt, she turned round and watched me stumbling forward, eyes very clearly pointing down at her inner thighs. I didn't even notice her stop, so transfixed was I by her heavenly legs. I stumbled right into her and grabbed her to stop myself falling over. My hand slammed straight into her chest and for one glorious moment it was right on her breast. She screamed in anger and kicked me as hard as she could in the shins. As I fell to the ground in agony she called me a dirty little creep and stormed off, leaving me writhing in blissful torment. It was the very first entry into my memory bank of sexual experiences. As inno-cent and clumsy as it was, it remains to this day the most exciting. It all went a bit pear-shaped from then on. She started going out with some blond hunk in the First XV and clearly told him about the little weirdo who followed her around and fondled her breast because he caught me in the library one day and gave me a good kicking. It didn't matter. What I had he could never take away. I'd had her first, in a fashion. I couldn't wait until O levels and more access to girls our age but until then my only outlet was the occasional tingle on a rope in gym class. I never forgot the blonde who went on to marry quite a well-known novelist. I found out about it and, despite myself, turned up at the wedding. It was a big mistake and I made a complete ass of myself. I did a bit of a *Graduate* and started bashing on the window and screaming and was eventually arrested. As I was being pushed into the police van I saw her looking at me. She definitely recognised me. They never forget.

School just became weirder and weirder. I genuinely felt that there was nothing useful for me to learn there.

Science freaked me out; after my very first physics lesson I knew that the only time that I would use anything taught to me in that lab was going to be in a Trivial Pursuit game and that I was going to forget the answer. Chemistry was simply guesswork. Almost everything that was discussed was so small that it was impossible to see or verify. Occasionally we would do some 'test' where we would mix things together and they would all froth up and explode but that was just showmanship to keep us interested; the actual facts could have been made up by the bass player in Procul Harem for all I knew. Biology was the worst; as far as I could see it was just an excuse for people to live out their vivisectionist fantasies by dissecting frogs and mice. Where did they get the frogs and mice from anyway? They obviously didn't catch them, so was there someone who delivered these creatures for that very purpose. What a career. Our biology teacher's big trick was to blow into a cow's lung to show us how they worked. I knew how they fucking worked, I had my own pair, but where did he get a pair of cow's lungs from and what the fuck did the teacher's wife make of all this?

Other weird subjects like maths and Latin left me similarly unstimulated. Unless you planned to live on an island and ignore the march of time we all had a calculator so what was the point of learning maths? It was a bit like teaching us to suck up dust from a carpet using our mouths. We could definitely do it, but why bother when we had a vacuum cleaner?

One holiday I couldn't go back to Lebanon as the civil war had got really bad and the airport was closed. A boy that I didn't know too well and who lived in Mozambique asked me whether I fancied coming to stay with him and his family for the holidays. I checked with my parents and they were fine about it and so three days later I found myself on a flight to Africa. I never really thought about why he had invited me – I just thought it might be a laugh. Little did I know.

On arrival in the capital I had to take a small plane up to their town. As we flew low over mile upon mile of jungle deep into the heart of darkness, I started to wonder what I had got myself into. I was met by the boy and his parents and immediately knew that I had made an enormous mistake.

The mother looked like the sort of woman that they cast as concentration-camp guards, the kind that always ends up being killed in a horrible way after having been unspeakably cruel to people so that the death is justified in movie morality. The father was a six-foot-six Boer who, strangely, had been kicked out of South Africa and had settled in Mozambique. He loathed the British and only sent his son to school there because the wife's parents were paying for it. He had a bright-red face discoloured by years of sun, drink and a vicious temper. We drove in virtual silence to their 'compound', a two-storey tin building surrounded by eight-foot walls and barbed wire. 'Security', I was told, was a big problem and I was never to leave the compound without an escort and I must not talk to 'bleecks' under any circumstance.

Things didn't improve at supper. I was famished but for moral reasons I had been a vegetarian for over two years. An enormous piece of blackened meat was thrust in front of me – and nothing else. When I told the father that I was a vegetarian, he stood up, went bright purple and started screaming about Communists and faggots, threw his plate against the wall and stormed out. I went to bed as early as I could, starving and slightly freaked out. I tried to read for a couple of minutes before succumbing to my brain's deep longing for sleep. I turned over and pulled the string hanging down next to my bed to turn the light off. That's when it all went very wrong. A piercing siren went off all over the house and lights started flashing on and off in the garden. I peered out of the window just in time to see the father, dressed only in his underpants, stalking around the perimeter wire carrying an enormous shotgun. Realising that I must have set off some panic alarm, I jumped back into bed and pretended to be asleep only moments before the concentration-camp guard burst into my room and asked me whether I had pulled the alarm cord. I pretended to have just woken up and denied it all. She was clearly not convinced but the alarm was switched off and I tried to get some sleep.

The next morning I was presented with another hunk of unidentifiable meat for breakfast that I was again unable to eat. For the rest of the morning the family hung around the pool and totally ignored me. I was starving and finally managed to sneak into the kitchen without anyone seeing me. I opened the fridge to find nothing but racks and racks of meat. I was about to close the door when I spotted a small drawer at the bottom. I pulled it open to find, to my delight, an enormous bar of Cadbury's Fruit and Nut chocolate. I snapped off two small chunks and scurried off to my room to savour it. My appetite sated, I returned to the pool where I spent the rest of the morning listening to the father tell the mother some story about 'fecking bleecks' stealing stuff from some mine he appeared to be involved in. About lunchtime there was a commotion from inside the house and the cook came out and launched into a tirade about something. We were all ordered into the sitting room by the father where all the staff were assembled. 'Somebody has stolen the fecking chocolate! There is a thief among us and when I catch them I'll cut their bloody arms off,' screamed the father. I went totally cold. I felt everyone's eyes bore into me. I was going to die here in the middle of some bloody jungle miles from home. They would probably just chuck my body into the river for the crocodiles to eat and tell everyone back home that I had died in a car accident.

It would be so easy – maybe they had planned this all along, maybe I'd done something to the boy and this was all part of some elaborate plan. 'Come on then, who took the bloody chocolate, who is the bloody thief?' screamed the father, looking straight at me. I stayed silent, the panic growing inside me. If I owned up I'd be swinging from a tree in the back garden before I could say 'Nazi'. I knew that they all knew it was me but I wasn't going to crack, it felt like my only way out – name and number, nothing else. I was actually becoming quite delirious and the room was swimming in and out of focus. I started to feel really hot and then I passed out. It was a lucky escape. When I came to I was in another room and a doctor was leaning over me listening to my heartbeat through a stethoscope. 'It's malaria,' I heard him tell the camp guard. 'At least three weeks in bed.' I fell back into unconsciousness and had the most horrific dreams of my life involving the whole Nazi family throwing knives at me as I dangled over a river filled with crocodiles eating my legs off. I was in hell for a month, stuck in a small hot room and fed once a day by a surly cook who had probably been given a beating for the chocolate incident just in case. I didn't see a single member of the family for three weeks and then they all came in and told me that I would be flying back to the UK in a week. It was the longest week of my life. When I finally left and staggered onto the plane, I vowed never to complain about anything else ever again. It didn't last long but it was sincerely meant.

I never quite felt the same after that trip. I sometimes wondered whether I'd been poisoned or someone had done some voodoo on me. I had always been quite confident and social before but I knew that something had changed. I didn't feel like talking to anyone and became very withdrawn. I started playing dungeons and dragons and got very involved in the whole world of fantasy and role play. Old friends dropped by the wayside as the dungeons and dragons bunch were not seen as the coolest on the block. I started to have really bad nightmares. The school doctor thought that they might be malaria flashbacks but I knew that they were something else, something deep inside of me that I couldn't explain away. Arthur, my dog, started featuring prominently in the nightmares. He was always angry, really angry. He would pick out the name of some boy that had annoyed me that day and encourage me to get my revenge. At the beginning it was little stuff like shitting in his slippers or putting hydrogen peroxide into his shampoo. But soon the ideas became much more twisted and violent. One day I caught a boy in my dorm talking about me to another boy. It was obvious that they were talking about me because they went dead quiet the moment I walked into the room. I just made out the words 'little shithead' at the door and that was enough. I worried about it all day but Arthur brought me the solution. The next morning I rushed back to house from the dining hall, got a golf club and waited behind the door. As soon as the boy walked in I swung the club as hard as I could and cracked open his skull, putting him in hospital for three months and getting me rusticated for two weeks. Whatever you felt about Arthur's ideas, they were certainly effective. The boy never returned to school and I was afforded a certain distance by potential adversaries. I suppose that I was quite unpopular really but I knew no different so it didn't have that much of an effect on me. (Oaksey disputes this. He feels that the malaria probably did have some form of long-term effect on me. He says that this can happen if you get it during adolescence. He thinks that this might have been one of the root causes of my problems. I have no idea. I certainly didn't really have any problems for the rest of my time at school, or any friends.) When girls joined us things definitely changed. I was really interested in them and because their entrance percentage requirement was about seventy per cent as opposed to the boys' thirty, we were faced with a gaggle of very bright, sociable girls and we were forced to up our game a bit. I realised that the world of dungeons and dragons was not going to get me a girlfriend and I had a kind of overnight transformation. I became a rather crap New Romantic. A hint of eyeliner, badly dyed Sun-In hair and a tiny tie knot turned me into a stereotypical public school trendy try-hard. It worked. I snogged a girl called Paris and we went out together for most of the rest of my time at school. I finally lost my virginity to her in someone's grandmother's flat in Belgravia whilst my best friend was vomiting profusely in the bathroom having drunk both our bottles of Martini. Most people probably have a song that reminds them of the time. I have the sound of projectile vomiting and it never fails to bring back mixed memories. The evening was slightly marred by me finding the grandmother's prosthetic breasts hanging up in the cupboard. Having clipped the thing on, fuelled by post-coital adrenaline, I started dancing round the flat trying to wake my by now unconscious friend. It was at this moment that the owner of the prosthetic breasts, the mysterious grandmother, decided to visit her London flat. We were turfed out unceremoniously to the screams of the wretched woman, who tried to get the doorman of her building to beat us up. Luckily we had previously eased our entrance into the flat with a bottle of whisky. He let us go.

Paris and I broke up about a week before A levels and she started going out with one of my best friends. There is nothing quite so intense as your first real heartbreak and Arthur visited me many times over that period. I heard from her about two years ago once I had got onto the telly. She was working as an account manager for a company that sold bathroom taps to Nigeria. I was very polite and asked her about her life and whether she was happy. She clearly wasn't. I downplayed my life and came off the phone curiously happy. Sometimes revenge is a strangely subdued affair. Despite my romantic trauma I did manage to do quite well in my A levels and school was finally over. I walked through the gates out into the great wide world. I was a free man at last. I could do anything I wanted. The world was my oyster. Carpe diem and all that. It all felt very big and scary.

The Road to Morocco

IT SEEMED TO be customary amongst my peers to take a year off before going to university. No one really had any explanation why. There were whispers about how it really 'improved' you and how it was a chance to do some charity work but it seemed pretty obvious to me that it was an excuse to go somewhere hot and get drunk. Once, it had been India where you got incredibly high and experimented with various forms of 'enlightenment' before returning home and forgetting all about it after boring people in the pub about 'how materialistic' they all were for a couple of weeks. By the time I came to leave school things had moved on. Everyone was off to Thailand. They were still all after the same thing but there was more getting high and a little less 'enlightenment' available. That suited everyone fine and in Phuket, Phukyou and Phukeverything 'full moon parties' were the order of the day.

I'd certainly never fancied the idea of India and Thailand seemed even duller. I liked the idea of getting away from everyone, not all meeting up somewhere twenty degrees hotter. Also no one seemed to want me to travel with them or meet up but that was not really a contributing factor.

I'd always liked the idea of Morocco. I'd just read some Paul Bowles and it sounded magical. I bought an Inter-Rail ticket that gave you unlimited travel on trains throughout

Europe and, for some reason, included Morocco. Politicians may not have been convinced that it was part of Europe but clearly train moguls felt that there was a link. The Inter-Rail ticket sounded fantastic: unlimited travel for around £100. The problem was that this just got you on the train, not anywhere to sleep. The grim reality of the Inter-Rail experience was days spent sleeping in boiling hot train corridors, drinking water from the loo and getting all your belongings stolen by German skinheads. It was actually not that far off what I imagined India to be like.

My first night was in Paris. The train pulled in at around eight in the evening and my next one left the following morning. I decided that I should sleep under the Eiffel Tower, which I think I considered quite a bohemian thing to do. As I was kipping down in the shadow of one of the huge concrete blocks beneath the tower, I met a couple of Americans who had been in Paris for about six months. They had some wine and I had some cigarettes and so we spent a couple of hours chatting very pleasantly. At about ten o'clock they produced a little flask of what looked like soup. They passed it round telling me that I would love it. It was magic mushroom soup and within minutes I was seeing everything in a slightly blurred form and starting to have some extraordinary hallucinations. The two Americans told me that they had found a way to climb up the tower and did I want to join them? I nodded hallucinatory approval and we were off. We climbed the enormous base block and hopped onto one of the staircases winding up the leg of the tower. About halfway up towards the first level we came to a locked door. They turned right and started shinning up the Meccano-style wall flanking the door. I followed slightly uncertainly and we managed to get high enough to shuffle across and drop down behind the locked door. We continued upwards towards the first floor viewing platform, my hallucinations becoming stronger and stronger, shadows becoming multi-jawed faces reaching out to pull me over the dark edges. I closed my eyes and continued on upwards, trying to cling onto my senses. We finally arrived on the first platform by climbing over another low, locked door. We sat down and had a celebratory cigarette and looked at the city of lights stretched out beneath our feet. We could see the New Opera House on Place de la Bastille, the Sacré Coeur up on Montmartre and the twinkling lights of the Champs Elysées leading off into the distance. The city was ours. Feeling like kings, we swigged more of the mushroom tea. At exactly one a.m., all the public lighting in the city gets turned off and we watched as a great wall of darkness enveloped the city. In a movie you would be alone with some gorgeous French girl who'd turn to you, lift her couture top to reveal perfect, pert breasts and whisper in sexy pidgin English, 'Do you see anything that you like?' We'd then spend the night making love before wandering down the banks of the Seine and sharing a coffee and a croissant at some romantic corner café. She would weep as I told her that I had to leave, I had to go to Morocco. She would accompany me to the train station and wipe away a beautiful tear as my train pulled out of the station. At the last moment she would give me a little silver ring that I would keep and treasure throughout my adventures in North Africa. Later I would return to Paris and we would meet again under a chestnut tree near the Sorbonne and I would decide to stay in Paris. We would live together in a studio apartment where she would continue her modelling career and I would become a wildly successful experimental artist. But this was no Richard Linklater construction and I, along with thousands of other spotty youths, was not living the dream. The reality was that I was halfway up an enormous metal lamp stand, off my nuts on mushrooms with a couple of Americans from Upper Sandusky in Ohio. I was suddenly very cold and mild paranoia took hold. I started to panic about the enormity of the world and what my place in it would be. Bidding farewell to my fellow adventurers, I made my way down, found some bushes, got into my sleeping bag and tried to get some sleep.

Morning came suddenly as I woke to find a man attempting to cut through the straps attaching me to my rucksack. I jumped up and tried to look threatening but he ambled off looking completely unhassled. I checked my belongings and hotfooted it to the train station. There was no sign of any doe-eyed lovely waiting to see me off so I clambered on the creaky old train and found my spot in the corridor just next to a blocked loo. Ah well! At least it was only a fifteen-hour journey. As the train roared through France and into Spain, the heat became unbearable. To make things that little bit better some bright spark had bought a can of CS gas in a Parisian shop. One of the joys of France for a youngster is the array of shops selling air pistols, large sheath knives and CS gas. This kind of store is a dream destination for any teenager. I think the girl had intended to use it for self-defence but she managed to let it off whilst showing it to her friend and the air quickly became unbreathable. Everyone panicked and started to push for the connecting door to the next carriage. One girl vomited everywhere as the scrum of backpackers rushed for fresh air. The conductor in the next carriage heard the commotion and, thinking that we were all trying to force our way into first class, locked the door. For the next seven hours I lay with thirty-two other teenagers in a corridor reaching temperatures of over 100 degrees Fahrenheit, breathing in the pungent smell of vomit and CS gas. Never had people been happier to see Algeciras, normally viewed as the arsehole of Spain. We spilled from the train of hell and drank ourselves into a stupor in the shitty little bars that surrounded the ferry port.

This was the main crossing point from Europe to North Africa, just up from the Pillars of Hercules and after a couple of beers things started to look a little bit brighter.

The ferry slipped away from the Spanish shore at seven the next morning and I spent the short trip up on deck watching Europe disappear as Africa rose up to greet us. The ship crept into Tangier harbour, the city glaring down at us from the surrounding hills. The dock was a riot of strange smells, mangy stray dogs, men in long gowns with little pointy hoods, kids running amongst us rubbing their bellies and holding out their hands for money. On the beach just to the left sat two rather forlorn-looking camels proffering a photo opportunity. Next to them lay three Moroccan women in full purdah, with only their eyes showing through the thin slits of their chadors. They were watching two Scandinavian girls go a bright shade of red as they lay on the beach in tiny bikinis. As I walked towards a waiting rank of taxis I was accosted by a multitude of dodgy-looking individuals offering accommodation for the night. Fortunately I had done some research and had decided to treat myself on my first night in Africa. I caught a taxi and wound my way up the twisty little lanes to the top of the hill where the Rif Palace Hotel awaited me. It had clearly been something fairly lovely about fifty years ago. Perhaps Noël Coward had supped a cocktail or two on the terrace during *la belle époque*, as my guide assured me he had but it was clear that we were currently in a very different '*époque*' possibly prefaced by something like '*terrible*' or '*triste*'. The place was a dump but I was exhausted and at least it had a roof and a room and I needed a treat like that before heading off south.

I soon realised that I was the only guest in the place and that my arrival had rather upset the two members of staff. From my room I could see a plateau of roofs festooned with rusty television aerials and lines of washing. In the corner I could see the hotel swimming pool, empty apart from a two-inch pile of leaves surrounding the greenish puddle of water covering the bottom. I wandered down the empty corridors, negotiated the crumbling staircase and entered the once splendid dining room. It was enormous and completely empty save for three tables in the far corner. I sat at what might once have been a bar and waited. Fifteen minutes later no one had come and I climbed over the bar and found two bottles of Moroccan beer and bit the tops off. I instantly felt better. With no sign of food I decided to head into the medina and do a bit of exploring. I walked through the deserted reception, through the barren front garden and out into the narrow street. I followed the twisty road back down into the main part of the city.

One of the first little places that I saw was a tailor shop

with a sign in the window proclaiming that 'I finess tailor in Tangier, cloths for gentleman and lady make it measure'. I couldn't resist.

I was after some comfy clothes that would be more suitable for the heat. I went in and a small fat man made me sit down and have some mint tea with him while we decided what it was that I was after. 'Hello, I speak Englaish, I learn tow years Oxford Universitt. I have beautiful hands for cloths.' He showed me his long, rather elegant, piano player hands and smiled a toothless smile.

'I need a couple of pairs of loose cotton trousers and four cotton shirts please,' I smiled back.

'No, no, not cotton, you Moroccan way, you best togs kit up supper please,' he continued rather mystifyingly.

'Just four cotton shirts, blue or white, and two pairs of black loose cotton trousers please,' I repeated, pointing to my trousers and shirt helpfully.

'Many men come, London bus, make good uniform, I make very best Savile Row,' he beamed. I gave up and asked for a price.

'You pay, you like on service, only very best Moroccan, you like.' And he shook my hand, indicating that we had indeed made a deal the details of which only he was privy to. I told him that I was off for a wander around the medina and then to get something to eat. 'Three clocks, no problem, I quick maker,' he muttered whilst pulling a measuring tape very tightly around my thigh.

'Fine I'll be back in three hours, OK?'

'No problem,' he said and I put down my empty glass of tea and wandered outside where a small crowd of boys had gathered. They all stood rubbing their bellies and reaching out but before I could put my hand in my pocket the tailor rushed out and smacked the nearest one very hard with a large stick. The boy went flying and ended up crumpled by the far wall. He and the whole group fled round the corner without even looking back.

'They lazy dogs, Cheitan, shame to me, apologies.'

I walked off rather embarrassed, unable to work out how to explain that I didn't need a psychopathic tailor as a bodyguard.

I found a small café type establishment and spent the next three hours playing chequers with a stoned German who had been in Tangier for over nine months. His name was Gerhard and he spoke pretty good English. Gerhard's parents were well-meaning hippy types who had apparently never really let go of the Sixties. He grew up in a small town near Munich where his parents were both teachers. His dad had been the headmaster of the local high school and his mother had been a primary school teacher. Gerhard said that he loved both his parents greatly but it had been a struggle growing up.

He'd been to England once on an exchange trip. He'd had to stay with a family in Rochester and the whole experience had clearly left him scarred. The grandfather had been killed in the Western desert by a German infantry attack and this had left the orphaned father with a hatred of foreigners and of Germans in particular. The mother thought that Europeans were unhygienic and had stapled plastic sheeting to everything in his room from the table to the bed. Gerhard said that it was a bit like living in a plastic bag for two weeks. The family had an older son who, when he wasn't busy in his main occupation of football hooliganism, would spend the evenings throwing darts from his bedroom window at Gerhard who had taken to sitting in the garden to lessen the chances of actual social contact. The word 'Nazi' had been sprayed on his bedroom door on his first morning there and Gerhard was never sure whether this was a symbol of respect from the right-wing hooligan or hatred from the xenophobic father. The final straw came when he observed both father and son demolishing the neighbour's new Volvo with hammers because they were under the impression that it was made in Germany. Why these people had ever wanted an exchange student was a mystery to Gerhard but he eventually upped sticks and left to spend the rest of his time in the UK sleeping in Hyde Park and eating left-over hot dogs from the bins around the Serpentine. He had never gone abroad again until now and he was clearly quite nervous about meeting another Englishman. The English family's other son who had gone to stay with Gerhard's family had been sent home after trying to burn down a local school because there were 'fucking Turks' hanging around there. Apparently, 'the Turk is almost worse than the German, they fucked my granddad up in the desert.' No one could be bothered to tell him that his granddad had been in what was now Libya. Gerhard was doing a PhD in Berber music and was in Morocco to attend an institute in the Atlas Mountains where some ex-pop star was teaching traditional North African drumming techniques. We parted on good terms and I promised to look him up if I made it that far.

I wandered back to the tailor's who had indeed whipped up a couple of outfits for me. He proudly produced two shiny pairs of what could only be called 'crap catchers', huge, baggy pantaloons made from a form of viscosey material normally reserved for a Greek's suit. The tops weren't much better. A shapeless, three-holed piece of material with some Arab squiggles ironed onto the back. I had no idea what they said but had a vague suspicion that it might be something along the lines of 'I went to Tangier and all I got was this Moroccan clown outfit.' I paid up, vowing to bin the lot as soon as possible and left.

On my return, the hotel seemed even more deserted than when I'd arrived. As I got to the reception area I noticed that all the doors had bits of wood hammered into them to prevent access. I couldn't get upstairs to my room so wandered out into the garden where a lone gardener was on his way out of the front gates with a bag of plants in his hands.

'Where is everyone?' I asked.

'Hotel closed, police finish,' he replied, making a beeline for the street.

'What do you mean it's closed? I'm staying here, all my stuff is up there.'

'You go now, police come back, take you to prison.' He slipped out through the gate and disappeared up the street.

I went back into the hotel and managed to tear the wood off the entrance to the stairs. The door to my room was wide open and it was completely empty – I had nothing left but what I'd taken with me, just my passport, about forty pounds sterling and the two Moroccan clown costumes. Things weren't looking too good.

I went back into town and eventually found what looked like the police station. I managed to talk to the heavily armed man sitting behind a dirty desk smoking a very smelly Moroccan cigarillo.

'I was staying at Rif Palace Hotel and all my stuff has gone and there is no one there. What can I do?' I asked slowly.

The man looked at me suspiciously.

'You stay at Rif Palace Hotel?' he asked.

'Yes,' I replied. 'All my belongings have been stolen and there is no one there.'

'You like Moroccan boys?' he asked threateningly.

'I've got nothing against them,' I replied carefully.

'You make movie Moroccan boys, you Cheitan, you give passport, you big problem.' He got up and called through to someone in the next room. There was no answer and he went through a door into the back room.

I had absolutely no idea what was going on or what I was about to be implicated in but it appeared unlikely that I was about to be handed the keys to Tangier so I hotfooted it out of the place and headed straight for the railway station. Tangier clearly wasn't my kind of town. I bought a ticket with some of my remaining money and, without knowing where I was headed, squeezed into a packed compartment and decided to see where fate would take me.

Fifteen hot hours later we pulled up in Marrakesh. I got out and walked into town. I needed somewhere to stay so that I could work out what the hell I was going to do next and how I was going to make some money. I wandered around the Djemma El Fna, the inappropriately named Square of the Dead that was the living epicentre of the city. It was like a scene from *The Arabian Nights*: food stalls, snake charmers, water sellers, child acrobats and a solid mass of humanity all moving en masse as though circling the

Kabbalah. It was fiercely hot and I escaped into a café on the square advertising rooms.

'What is your cheapest room?' I asked the man behind the bar.

'Very cheap, cheapest in Marrakesh. You British, you like Michael Winner?' he asked in a glorious non-sequitur.

'No, I don't but I need a room, very cheap,' I continued.

'Come, I show you nice room, very cheap.' He got up and ushered me down some stairs hidden by the entrance to the bar. We descended into the depths of the building and he pushed open a door that was barely hinged and entered a damp, dark little room. In the corner was what passed for a bed with a single dirty sheet on it. There were no windows but at eye level was a grille that clearly went into the bar as I could see the bare feet of several customers and occasionally a fag end would be blown through the space and land on the bed.

'You like? Five dinars, very cheap,' he exclaimed proudly. I didn't have too much choice so I handed over the money and settled down to try and get some sleep. I wondered what the link to Michael Winner might be. Maybe he had shot the prison scene from *Death Wish IV* in here. Maybe he had given one of the owner's cousins' restaurants a bad review and had been imprisoned in here until he apologised. I was never to find out.

The next day, my own clothes filthy and sweaty, I was forced to don my clown's outfit. As I crossed the square, it seemed that the entire population of Marrakesh was laughing at me, like one of those dreams where you are naked in public and everyone is staring at you and you've nowhere to hide. Mind you, I think I would have preferred to be naked. I decided to leave town and set out for the Atlas Mountains to try to find Gerhard and stay with him until I could get some money wired out and get home. He had given me the name of the village of Ouirgane.

I managed to hitch a lift on the roof of a tractor, mainly because the driver was in such paroxysms of mirth at my attire that he wanted to show everyone he knew the twat he'd picked up. He kept stopping and yelling to people in buildings and shops to come out and they would all have a good laugh at me before we moved on to the next. About six hours later we crawled into Ouirgane. I climbed gingerly off the tractor and graciously allowed the driver to borrow a camera from a friend and to take a series of photos of me before I went on my way. I left him and a group of cackling locals and walked into the village.

Asking around, I was told that the drumming institute was just two miles out of the village up a rough track. I hitched up my crap catchers and started to walk. Half an hour later I arrived outside a large gate sporting a handwritten sign that announced that this was the 'Atlas Rhythm Corporation'. Underneath the title were written the words 'If you ain't got riddim then you ain't geddin' in.' I was already dreading what I was going to find inside but, having no other options, I knocked and waited. In the distance I could make out a banging sound as though someone was doing some building work. After a couple of minutes a small hatch in the door was slid open and a weathered, tanned face peered out at me. The smell of BO was quite overpowering.

'Yeah, what do you want?' snarled the human armpit.

'I'm a friend of Gerhard and he asked me to pop in if I was in the area,' I whimpered.

'You look more like a friend of Dorothy in that outfit, dude,' laughed the human cesspit.

'Can I come in?' I pleaded. There was a long silence, then the sound of a large bolt being wrestled free and the gates opened.

I found myself face to face with the bastard son of Keith Richards and Jimmy Hendrix. He was clearly no fan of constriction – everything he wore flowed, tumbled and hung off his scrawny body.

'I'm Kaj,' he muttered. 'Follow me,' and he wandered off towards a two-storey terracotta-coloured building which a group of people were sitting in front of banging away on what looked like a collection of pots and pans. The cacophony subsided as we approached and I immediately spotted Gerhard and gave him a wave. He looked rather surprised to see me but got up and shook my hand. He introduced me to the rest of the rhythm section.

'This is Will, Rupert, Dave, Kate, Anna and Kirsten.' I shook them all by the hand as they looked me up and down, barely suppressing a group giggle at my outfit. Rupert, a Jim Morrison lookalike, stood up and in a very clipped tone asked me to call him Abu Shakra. The others then all chipped in with their 'Atlas' names and the list started to sound like a roll call in a Notting Hill Gate primary school. After a couple of minutes of pleasantries, Gerhard offered to show me the sleeping quarters and I followed him into the terracotta building. As soon as we got inside he turned to me and asked me whether I was a homosexual. I assured him that I was not but he looked uncertain and asked me why I had followed him here. I told him my story and he visibly relaxed and took me upstairs to show me two rooms with bunk beds in them.

The 'Institute' was free but was run a bit like a kibbutz – everyone had to chip in and drumming class was compulsory.

'The boys are all English public school boys and very racist, they keep mentioning the war – it is happening all over again. What is wrong with your country?' asked Gerhard. I told him not to worry, it was just the way things were in England; we could never let anything go and recent penalty shoot-outs didn't help stuff. They'd get bored of it soon. Gerhard told me that 'Kaj' used to be a very big-name musician and had played for bands like Yes and Marillion and had once even played with the Rolling Stones.

'The Rolling Stones?' I asked, slightly incredulous.

'Yes, he stood backstage and played bass while Bill Wyman got girls' phone numbers from the crowd. He pretty much played the whole set. Afterwards he got into a fight with Keith Richards and he keeps a piece of his shirt with Keith's blood on it attached to his necklace.'

'Cool,' I said, wondering if the rest of his clothes were of a similar age.

That evening, after supper of couscous and vegetables we retired to the drumming room, a long dark room with a bench along the whole of one side. Littered around the room were various implements none of which really resembled anything that I knew as a drum. We all grabbed an item and the idea was simply to bang away in unison and, according to Kaj, we would find 'a communal rhythm'. Needless to say nothing of the kind occurred and for the next two hours we must have scared away every wild animal within two miles of the compound. Finally, with no discernible signal from Kaj, the session drew to an end and we all lay around exhausted as someone passed a very strong joint round. After a couple of drags everything suddenly seemed a whole lot better and I started talking to Kirsten and Dave, or 'BoomBhaji' and 'Solaris 1', as they preferred to be known. I was christened 'Baggyone' in honour of my outfit and as a very weak pun on Bhagwan. They all found this hilarious and the evening rolled on in a similar vein. I explained my predicament and that I had, frankly, had quite enough of Morocco and needed to get back to the UK but had to get some money first. Kaj's ears pricked up and he budged over to where we were sitting.

'Maybe I can help you with your problem,' he said. 'We'll talk about it in the morning.' This was very good news and I eventually slumped into a stoned sleep where I dreamed of being chased down Oxford Street by naked Hare Krishnas who wanted to make me their new god as they admired my crap catchers so much. I couldn't really run very fast in them and ended up jumping down a manhole to get away from them. Down in the darkness sat Arthur and he was very angry. 'The bloody cat's only gone and had kittens and now they're everywhere. What am I supposed to do when the whole place is filled with pussy? I can't take much more of this.' He was holding a large revolver in his front left paw and had it pointed at his temple. 'I'm gonna bloody blow myself away,' he bellowed.

'Don't do it,' I screamed. 'Put the gun down, Arthur.' I woke up with a jolt to find Kirsten lying next to me.

'Who's Arthur?' she whispered, stroking my head. 'Anyone I should be worried about?' I tried to focus, was this actually happening to me? The whole hippy cliché of beautiful German free love lady offering herself to me within hours of meeting her? This was better than what might have happened in Paris, I thought, trying to remain calm.

'Arthur is my talking dog, he was my only friend for about four years when I was a kid,' I whispered, trying to make it all sound a bit weird and sexy. Her hand stopped stroking my head and she looked me straight in the face.

'You had a talking dog for a friend when you were a kid?' she asked quizzically.

'Yeah but don't worry about it . . . it's all a bit difficult to explain but ever since I've been little I've felt that I'm really special, that I kind of had magical powers and was destined to rule over other men . . .' Jesus, I was really stoned and talking utter bollocks. I could only hope that my megalomaniac mutterings would appeal to the German in her.

'You are weird, really weird, Baggyone, but I like that, I really like that.' It seemed to have done the trick. She started stroking my head again and her other hand started playing with the buttons of my crap catchers. What a result, it was going to happen just like in the rubbish films.

'Solaris, you have eyes like a cow,' I whispered, immediately realising that this probably didn't quite sound as I intended it to. 'I mean that you have big dopey eyes and I really like hairy armpits whereas a lot of Englishmen don't. I think it's very . . . natural.' Christ, was I on some sort of truth drug or something? Just shut up and let her fingers do the walking. But I couldn't, the dope was too strong. I could only see Arthur's big slobbery face right in front of me, and he was laughing: 'What the hell are you doing? You were born for better things than this, she's a bloody Kraut, get a grip, punch her in the face, go on, remember Coventry.'

I wasn't really sure what Arthur was going on about but a sharp pain caused by Kirsten's teeth gently nibbling my earlobe was enough. I jumped up, throwing her across the room, shouted something about going over the top to spear the Hun and ran out of the room. It wasn't the best seduction technique; Kirsten shouted something after me about all the English being the same and that we should just come out with it and stop pretending. I lapsed into a stoned coma and slept for a good ten hours under a tree outside.

When I woke up, I went inside. The drumming room was empty but I could hear conversation coming from the dining room. I wandered in and joined the rest of the group for a breakfast of yoghurt and honey. After breakfast some of the group went outside to practise 'Tantric' drumming. I decided to pass on the opportunity as, surprisingly, did Kaj. He joined me in the orchard area for a cigarette, clearly with something on his mind.

'I know that you want to go back to the UK but have little bread, yeah?' he asked.

'That's right. I might be able to get some wired out but I don't really want to ask anyone for anything – I'm supposed to be proving myself out here although I'm not entirely sure to whom or what about,' I replied hesitantly.

'OK, well, I have a problem that you could help me with and which would allow you to get back to the UK. Are you interested?' I nodded and he continued.

'I have a friend in London, Nick Bakeman, you know him? He was the main guy in Balsamic Tentacles for a while before joining me in T-Bone Socket. Man, we were the main cats for a couple of years back then.' His eyes narrowed as he started to drift back to the halcyon days when prog-rock was king and the triple album was considered restrained.

'To be honest, Kaj, it wasn't really my bag, but I know people who loved that sort of stuff.'

'Don't tell me you haven't heard of Joe Van Cliff, played with Satriani for a while?' he pleaded.

'Oh sure, he was the bollocks, really great . . . stuff,' I replied gingerly, hoping he wouldn't probe too much further.

'Cool, well, Nick is a good mate of Joe's and I promised him that I come to London with two Berber toe drums that he wants to use for new project he's doing. He's got this big corporate gig doing the big march re-launch thing at Thorpe Park. It's not really his thing but it's good bread, you know? Anyway, he wants to give things a bit of ethnic vibe, kind of take it away from whole mittel-europ style, do you know what I mean?'

I didn't but nodded enthusiastically as I smelled a free lunch.

'Also I humping that Kirsten bird and English all signed on for another month's course. Looks like my riddim stick is going to be being used quick quick.' He laughed in a particularly unattractive way that suddenly aged him. Cut his hair and put him in a shirt and trousers that had a defined shape and he would have looked like a sixty-year-old geography teacher. At least I was now in no doubt as to who had written the dreadful verse on the front door.

'So anyway, I'm thinking if you take drums to Nick in London then maybe I deal with expenses. Interested?'

Too fucking right I was and we shook on it there and then. Things were suddenly looking up. I was to leave the following day and decided to try and enjoy my last night. It had dawned on me that I didn't really know why I had come to Morocco in the first place. It was full of no-hopers and I definitely wasn't going to join their slow descent into reefer madness. Even Kaj had clearly singled me out as someone he could trust, someone special – maybe Arthur was right. Maybe I did have some sort of special destiny awaiting me. I certainly didn't here. I had to return to England where I could fulfil whatever destiny awaited me. Maybe in a funny way I had learned something out here even if it was only that I wasn't cut out to be a stoned hippy. It was a start.

Kirsten didn't really speak to me all evening but what did I care? I was out of here and these people were soon to be mere eaters of my dust. I took part in a final percussion session where Kaj encouraged us to 'loosen up' by all trooping out into the orchard and smashing the tree trunks with kitchen implements whilst yelling out any words that came to mind when we thought of our parents. I was surprised to see Gerhard hammering away at his lemon tree and I could just make him out amongst the nonsense being shouted by everyone else: '*Gott im Himmel*, flower power, Procul Harem, Peter, Paul *und* Mary, Maharishi, Beetle, Nudisch, moustache, *raus raus*, so many moustaches, Nuclear *nein danke*, peace man, tear down the wall, free love, our little secret, Uncle Ronnie's coming to stay, *ich liebe dich*, one day a real rain will come . . .'

His childhood had clearly touched on the darker side of the whole hippy thing. I didn't feel that it was my place to ask him about it but I hoped that he would find something here that helped him. He was all right, for a German.

Kaj drove me down to the outskirts of Marrakesh the next morning. He refused to drive into the city as he said that he had some 'issues' with the authorities and didn't want to get into any complications. I got out of his white Renault 4 and he handed me the two drums wrapped tightly together with an envelope for his friend with the address written on it. He shook my hands and handed me two hundred dollars.

'Thanks for doing this, man, and no tough feelings about Kirsten, she told me about the scene the other night.'

'Yeah, she was pretty wasted and I knew that she was your woman so I hung back; it was no problem, man,' I lied.

'She has a thing for virgins so you did nice to fight her off. I'll see you around.' Kaj chuckled and gunned the motor and the little Renault puttered off back up the steep road leading into the Atlas.

'I'M NOT A VIRGIN . . .' I shouted at the disappearing car, but he couldn't hear me and I just got funny looks from a couple of backpackers walking past me on the other side of the road.

'Don't vorry, he didn't look that much of a catch,' shouted one of them, giggling.

'Fuck off,' I shouted cleverly before starting to walk into town. I was well shot of the lot of them.

I boarded the train for Tangier and squeezed into a crowded compartment by persuading a woman to move her goat and took a seat in the corner by the window. It was midday and I was starving, I hadn't had any breakfast and I eagerly dipped into the bag of goodies I'd been given at the compound. I was busy buttering an enormous slice of Arab bread and layering it with some labneh and olives when I suddenly noticed that the whole compartment had gone silent. I looked around and saw that everyone's eyes were focused intently on my sandwich.

Finally an elderly man leaned over and told me that it was the month of Ramadan and that everyone was fasting during daylight. It would obviously be very bad form for me to munch down a meal whilst everyone else was starving. I put the food back in the plastic bag and sat looking out of the window trying not to think about fat steaks and hamburgers.

'When the sun goes down we will all share food and there will be much feast, Hamdillah,' smiled the elderly man at me before returning to some pathological fiddling with his worry beads.

The day dragged on and on. At one point hunger seemed to play tricks with everybody's digestive systems and an impressive sonata of burps and farts filled the compartment with a heavy stench that added to the already unsufferable heat. As we approached the foothills of the Rif mountains the sun began to set and the mood in the gas chamber lifted somewhat. Everyone produced food from little plastic bags kept under the bench seats. I took out my half-made sandwich and was about to tuck in when I noticed that everyone was offering their stuff to everyone else first. I proffered my sandwich half-heartedly to the man sitting next to me. He beamed, nodded a thank you and grabbed the whole thing, wolfing it down in seconds. I sat twiddling my fingers for a while wondering what to do when the lady opposite me, veiled to the eyebrows, offered me a bowl of something that looked a bit like soup. I took it gratefully and, using a bit of bread that my neighbour had given me, started to tuck in. It had a thick velvety consistency and was surprisingly warm. It had a funny taste, somewhere between leek and potato soup and vomit. As the first mouthful slid down my throat I realised that I was going to have great difficulty keeping it down. The man opposite helpfully informed me that this was a Marrakeshi delicacy, always eaten during the month of Ramadan.

'It is purée of sheep's brain, very good for fun with woman.' I looked at him and then down into the bowl, feeling bile rise in my throat.

'Excuse me,' I muttered and got up and made a quick visit to what passed for a loo, a small room with no door consisting of a hole in the floor looking straight onto the track below. I soon felt a bit better and returned to the carriage. Everyone seemed to have finished their meals and were putting them away. I was now starving, desperate for something to take away the taste of mashed brains. In the corner opposite me, a small man was still eating. His eyes flitted from one person to another as though daring them to ask for any of his supply. I fixed him with a determined stare and every time he looked my way made it very obvious that I was after some of his rather delicious-looking kebab sandwich. He finally gave in and made a feeble attempt to offer his remaining roll. I nodded gratefully and grabbed it. The smell was orgasmic and, actually salivating, I let the heady mix swirl around my nasal passages for a moment. Suddenly the sliding door of the compartment was flung open to reveal a grotesque figure. It was a woman of indeterminate age, wearing nothing but filthy rags and carrying an equally unattractive baby. She stuck her claw-like hand out into the middle of the carriage and pleaded for money from its unimpressed occupants. Realising that she wasn't getting anywhere with the locals, she fixed her attention on me and homed in for the kill. She jabbered on at me, hand outstretched, eyes blazing like a witch from *Macbeth*. The man who'd told me about Ramadan butted in and explained that she was asking me for money as she was pregnant and already had two children. I tried to look sympathetic but told the man to tell her that I had no money. He did so and she looked very unimpressed. She jabbered on again and the man told me that she wanted to know whether I was calling her a liar. The whole compartment was watching now. I asked the man what she thought I was accusing her of lying about. He answered that she thought I didn't believe she was pregnant. Before I could answer she put her baby on the floor of the compartment, lifted a rag and produced a single enormous bosom. She grabbed it with a clammy long-nailed hand and squirted a long stream of breast milk straight at me. The milky missile hit me right in the face and covered my kebab in a thin residue of stinky liquid. There was a long silence and then the compartment erupted in laughter. The woman picked up her unfortunate baby and, screaming obscenities at me, took her leave to try her luck elsewhere. I wiped the milk off my face and held the soaking kebab slightly hesitantly in my lap. I was about to dump it in what passed for a bin when the small man waved at me and took it back. He wolfed it down in three mouthfuls. I spent the rest of the trip between the corridor and the bathroom.

The train pulled into Tangier at about three in the morning. I decided to head for the beach and try to get some kip there and then make my way to the airport the following morning. I found a group of backpackers doing the same thing and managed to get about four hours of relatively undisturbed sleep apart from the sounds of rutting from a Swedish couple about twenty feet away.

I spent four precious dollars on a cab to the airport where, for almost the first time since I arrived in Morocco, I was in luck. There was a flight to London in four hours' time and the ticket would cost me one hundred and twenty dollars, leaving me with enough to get something to eat and drink in the airport café. I popped into the newsagent to buy an English newspaper. As I was paying for a two-day-old copy of *The Times* I noticed a headline on the *Journal de Tangier*, the local French-language newspaper. The headline read '*Hotel Porno Scandale, les autorités cherchent toujours l'evadé anglais.*' I grabbed the paper and sat on a bench to read the whole article. It announced that the gay porn film ring had been smashed as police raided the hotel in Tangier where the filmmakers would use local boys in hardcore porn films destined for the European market. Apparently the police had got everyone except for the shady leader of the gang, a young Englishman who had just made his escape, having actually turned up at the police head-quarters to taunt the officers involved in the case. I stood up and immediately binned the newspaper. They didn't seem to have a name for me and there was no picture but I had to get out of this bloody country before something else went wrong. I sat in the café and had a good meal and a couple of beers. I was hardly incognito because my clown costume was still causing much mirth amongst the locals but I was confident that I could make good my escape. Time crawled, but it was finally boarding time and the beers had given me a welcome lift. I had no bags, only the drums, so I checked in and went straight to the passport desk, resplendent in my crap catchers, carrying nothing but two Moroccan drums; I looked like the ultimate tourist casualty but I was going home and that was all that mattered for the moment.

I handed my passport over to the surly man behind the desk and he gave it a cursory glance, handed it back and nodded me through. I joined a small queue for the X-ray machine and started to imagine my first meal in the UK – I would go to Bertorelli's La Toscana and have a spag bog. Life would be so much better with some good British grub down me.

I walked through the machine carrying my bag. The soldier on the other side nodded me past, I was free. I could almost taste the spag bog. As I walked off I heard someone scream something. I kept walking but felt a hand rest on my shoulder. The soldier pulled me round and marched me back to the machine. I asked him what the problem was. He said nothing and spun me round again, indicating my back to the other officials. I asked the man again what the problem was.

'Why you wear this, you stupid bastard?' He pointed to my back again. I suddenly realised he was talking about the squiggles on the back of my clown costume.

'I don't know what it means, a tailor made it for me in Tangier. What does it say?' I was almost blubbering.

'It say that you like Pope, he smoke dope.'

I had nothing to say; the tailor had obviously translated something from some T-shirt he'd seen to amuse foreigners. I presumed that, being Moslems, they weren't fervent supporters of the Papacy but I could see why it would cause some suspicion.

The soldier frisked me and then grabbed my bag and put it on a plastic tray and gave it to a man next to another X-ray machine. My drums came through the machine and

I was about to pick them up when the man behind the screen shouted something to his mate next to me. He grabbed the drums and put them back through the machine. They all crowded round the screen and pointed at something and then looked up at me. A sinking feeling started to creep through me. They took the drums and me into a back room and asked me what was in them. I told them the story, knowing as I said it that I was fucked – how could I have been so stupid? Another man came in with a hammer and took a couple of blows to smash both frames open. Inside the drums in four neat plastic bags was a generous amount of Moroccan grass. I collapsed, both physically and mentally. I knew that nothing was going to get me off this one.

One week later I was listening through an interpreter to a Moroccan judge handing down his sentence. The lawyer told me that he had been very lenient considering and I got two years in Tangier Central Prison, known locally as 'the devil's arsehole'. About ninety per cent of the building, an old French arsenal, was underground. I will not go into detail of what happened to me in the nine months that I spent there. Suffice to say that I walked out blinking in the midday August sun a changed man. I hardly ever think back to those experiences although Oaksey has often encouraged me to. Even writing about it all makes my head spin. All I can say is that it has had a profound effect on my tastes and attitudes. I owe an enormous debt of thanks to my second cellmate Ahmed El-Bubba without whose friendship and, damn it all, love I would not have survived the experience. Thank you, Bubba, thank you for everything, you are an amazing man and I will be eternally grateful to you. Let's move on.

Dreaming Spires

I COULD HAVE walked into Oxford or Cambridge. There must have been a mix-up with the papers because I never got the invite. I wanted something a bit different anyway. Chalk Farm Polytechnic was perfect for me – established in 1982, it was a melting-pot of radicalism, drugs and people. I hated it pretty much from the start.

After Morocco I had spent a couple of months recovering in a small specialist hospital in Devon. I had become quite insular and withdrawn and found it hard to readjust to modern Western life. I found my salvation in an unexpected place: the world of Goth. I had always seen these curious creatures, all big black hair, black clothes, black make-up, moping around and was vaguely aware of the music they liked but knew little of their philosophy. A young Goth called Alan was in hospital with me and he taught me a lot about their lifestyle and philosophy. Their beliefs are deeply held but do tend to ostracise them from so-called normal society. They mix a love of French poetry with a penchant for the violin and the high Victorian influences of architecture and death to form a simple, digni- fied way of life. I found it very attractive. Two weeks after my discharge from hospital, I found myself sporting an unruly mop of back-combed blue-black hair, with a fondness for eyeliner and the music of Fields of the Nephilim, Sisters of Mercy and The Cure. Within a month I was down to just

20 mg of Valium. It just goes to show that modern medicine doesn't have all the answers.

Polytechnic life was not exactly what I had hoped for; a lot of the students were from a very different background to me, many had come from the North and were taking the opportunity to spend three years in the big city before returning to a lifetime down the mines. They were the salt of the earth and I loathed them.

In fact, it was proving quite difficult for me to really find anyone who totally understood me. Possibly I was a lot more mature than most and had been through a lot more stuff in my life. Some of them were very unpleasant, calling me 'posh cunt' and 'fucking Goth twat' whenever I wandered into the 'Muammar Gaddafi' bar area. I had found a really nice little basement bedroom in Baker Street to live in and for the first couple of months spent a lot of time there reading Baudelaire and writing my own poetry. Looking back, some of it wasn't too bad but I never really intended it to be read by anyone else. It was more of a mood thing, sitting in the candlelight, listening to 'Charlotte Sometimes' by The Cure and writing, always writing away on endless bits of paper. I found some of them the other day in a trunk; one really stood out and seemed to capture those times:

> Silent and Grey
> Sitting down here, eyes level with the street
> Sitting down here, no people to meet
> Sitting down here, all damn day
> Sitting down here, fucking silent and grey

Rather good even if I say so myself. Don't know what the grey was all about because I was really into black but it was probably something to do with the rhythm. Reading it all again has made me think about whether I should get the whole lot organised and maybe get them published.

Anyway, after a couple of months I made a decision that I was either going to get more involved at poly or leave. My degree was in Politics and I specialised in modern European city states like San Marino and . . . the other ones. It was fascinating but didn't exactly keep me busy and I didn't really get on with my tutor, Mr Munter. He was the type that felt that poly should be like school – you had to turn up, write essays, that sort of stuff, very old-fashioned for a supposedly 'modern' institution. I told him that my outlook was very different but he totally disrespected my feelings. We didn't really get on or see each other that much.

I decided to get proactive and become involved in the running of the place. My first thought was politics but it was all very Socialist Worker and Amnesty International type bleeding-heart stuff – lunatics frankly. So I changed tack and focused on the more social side of things. The entertainments officer was a powerful figure within the poly. They received a large amount of money every year to organise concerts and 'happenings' for which the poly was quite well known. They were particularly good at bringing unknown American bands over before they got big here in the UK. The post was up for election and so I decided to run. My campaign plan was to use the age-old political method of bribery to ensure my election. My manifesto promised a crisp ten-pound note to anyone who voted for me. I had recently been left quite a hefty sum of money by an aunt whom I'd never met. I think her husband had been incarcerated by the Yemenis in some secret-ops campaign. Someone in the family had told her of my problems in Morocco but not in great detail. I think she thought that I was some form of political prisoner because she sent me a rather moving letter about how very few young people took a stand like mine and that I was very brave and should be proud of myself. God knows what she had been told but it certainly paid off.

The election was a success. I won by a landslide that cost me £1500. Money well spent I thought, since I was now controlling an annual budget of over fifty thousand. I immediately retrieved my investment from the budget by claiming for a 'recce' trip to the USA that I never actually made.

The poly had quite a decent concert hall which was why it had become a good place for bands to play. I immediately used my influence to book two of my favourite bands, Zodiac Mindwarp and a cool band called Flock of Seagulls. I was determined that my first big event would be a success and actually worked quite hard on getting a large crowd in with a proper light show and even a sound mixer, something almost unheard of in most cheap student concerts. I had been lumbered with an American band that would also have to play on the night. I really didn't have much interest in Americans or their music but one of the budgetary stipulations was that we should always have an American band on the bill.

I was expected to look after this band for the two nights they were in London. Quite frankly I hadn't taken this job to be a nanny to a bunch of dopeheads from America but once again I had no choice since I was the only person employed by the Student Union. The last guy had about three people working with him and that had seemed like a criminal waste of money to me so I had shouldered all the responsibility (and salaries) myself.

I met them at Victoria coach station where they had just arrived on a bus from Belgium. They had been playing some weird festival and were all excited about their performance and how it had gone. They were an odd trio, a big-lipped, ponytailed drummer, a tall, thin, scruffy bassist and the oddly dressed blond singer who had a penchant for ladies' sunglasses and The Sex Pistols. It was typical really, Americans coming over and thinking that punk was still the big thing here – I half expected them to want to go to the King's Road and see the tourist punks. To their credit they didn't and I took them to the very cheap B & B that I'd booked them into in Shepherds Bush Road. They were actually all right, a bit childish at times and the singer was a bit moody but they weren't offensive. I tried to talk to them about music but they were either so retro or try-hard cool that it was an uphill struggle. The singer hadn't even heard of The Nephilim and didn't rate Zodiac Mindwarp. Just you wait, I thought to myself. Just you wait, Mister Yankee Doodle, until they blow you off stage, but I kept my own counsel. We spent a very dull day wandering around town, spending a couple of hours in Record Tape and Exchange buying old records before wandering around Hyde Park smoking spliffs and throwing bread at the ducks. I got quite stoned and battled long and hard to keep Arthur's voice out of my head. I can remember zoning in and out from the singer talking about some girl he'd fucked in Belgium who was coming over to see the gig and Arthur repeating over and over, 'use the knife, use the knife, destiny is in your hands', then back to the singer moaning on about how she was the best fuck in the world, then back to Arthur: 'use it, use it'. I was going to have to stop smoking this stuff.

We ended up in a café in Soho where endless espressos brought me back down to relative sanity. We talked about the gig that night and I explained that there were two other bands and that because of time they could only play five songs. The singer got really antsy about this but I put him in his place and told him that he was lucky to play anywhere. He was a reasonable guy and didn't give me any grief. I almost felt sorry for them – it was a thankless task touring, especially when you were at the very bottom. I left them in the café and headed off to the poly where I had to get everything ready. I told the Yanks to be there by seven or they wouldn't get on stage. I knew what musos were like. Come the evening and we had a big crowd, a really big crowd actually and Mr Mindwarp and The Seagulls were having a bit of a spat about who was headlining. I gave it to Mindwarp as he was older and I thought he had the best stage presence. I was beginning to enjoy my new power. The Americans turned up ten minutes before they were to go on stage, no sound check, nothing. They were a mess, barely had a tune to their name, just lots of angry loud guitar and unintelligible lyrics. The singer looked like he was in the throes of some sort of epileptic fit. The crowd got into them quite quickly, which was lucky as I needed to get The Seagulls on as soon as possible. After the fourth burst of noise I jumped on stage and whispered into the tall bassist's ear that this had to be the last one, so why didn't they play a cover, something everyone knew? He turned round and lamped me with his bass, sending me flying into the crowd who, like the drunks they were, cheered madly. I got up, bleeding heavily from my forehead and dragged myself over to the fuse box. I pulled the lever and the whole hall went dark at the same time as the music cut out. The band went nuts and I had to lock myself into my office before calling security and having them removed. When I returned to the hall there was a near riot going on and The Seagulls had been given a good going-over. Zodiac Mindwarp had left the building. It appeared that the American band had quite a dedicated following. What the fuck did they all know? I very much hoped that my path would never again cross with the aggressive trio with the ridiculous name, Nirvana. How they went on to become so big is beyond me. The following week I managed to book the remaining two members of Supertramp and we sold nearly forty tickets. Now that was proper music.

It was about this time that I decided to form a band myself. Coming into contact with so many bands had made me realise that this was something that I could actually do really well. I put an ad in a guitar shop in Denmark Street. I still have a copy of it. It reads:

WANTED – BUDDING ROCK STARS

Multi-talented singer, lyricist, poet seeks like-minded individuals to form and play in his band. Prepare to follow a genius.

Influences should range from:
Fields of the Nephilim to The Mission
Call Jazz – 01 348 0407
No time wasters or tossers

No one replied to it. I suspect that a lot of people were put off by my confidence. I had taken on the name Jazz – I thought it summed up my character, cool, outsider, freeform, tuneless, black, really succinctly. I started to ask people to call me Jazz instead of Dom but most didn't. A lot of people said that it sounded stupid but I loved it. I was Jazz and Jazz was me.

In the end my musical career came to me by chance, or even fate, as I prefer to think of it. I was in a pub called the Spice of Life off Cambridge Circus. It was a well-known Goth hang-out and I was sitting there supping a large Purple Nasty when a girl Goth came up to me and asked me whether I could sing. I told her straight up that yes, I could. It turned out that she was German, her name was Britte and she and two other German girl Goths had set up a little band and they wanted a male singer who also had to be a Goth, was I interested? I had a good feeling and, as this hadn't happened to me since I'd gone on Valium, I said yes immediately.

We met up for the first rehearsal in a studio beneath the railway arches under Putney Bridge station. The other two girls, Eva and Marlene, were pretty cool and I liked them all straight away. They weren't too bad as musicians either and were soon playing a pretty depressing version of The Cult's 'Rain'. We came up with a name for the band that night: The Big Black Dead, which I thought was good and, well, dark. We played for a couple of hours before ending up in a pub. This was going to be fun. We rehearsed three times a week and we were almost starting to sound pretty good. I wrote a couple of songs like 'Valium Lows' and 'Don't Rain On My Death Parade' that I really liked and we started to think about trying to get some recording done. We were even thinking about a gig or two.

One day I was sitting in the Mandela bar in the basement of the poly when a middle-aged man whom I'd occasionally seen hanging around the place came and sat down next to me. After a couple of minutes he asked me what my name was. I told him that I was Jazz Black (I like this surname, it was very me and I hardly ever used my real name any more) and he told me that his name was Douglas Philby and that he wanted to talk to me. Could he buy me a drink? Fairly sure that this was a gay pick-up, I decided to at least get a cider and black out of the situation before giving him the brush-off. He bought two drinks at the bar and returned to my table and sat down. He said that he represented a particular division of the government and wondered whether I'd thought about what I might do when I graduated. I told him that I hadn't really thought about it but I intended to do something musical and that I wasn't really a civil service kind of guy. He laughed and said that he'd kind of guessed that. He told me that he represented a section of the civil service that were interested in recruiting a slightly different sort of person from the classic Oxbridge linguist that they normally targeted. He said that it had been noted that I had been brought up in the Middle East and had spent some time in Morocco, 'a little longer than you expected'. He laughed and said that there was nothing to commit to straight away but he just wondered whether I would be interested in attending an interview sometime in the next two weeks. I hesitated but he said that they would pay all expenses for the day and I decided to give it a go. It wasn't like I was busy.

A week later I found myself outside an anonymous office block just north of Warren Street tube station. I rang the doorbell and the door clicked open. I walked into what looked like the reception area of a small firm of chartered accountants. Whatever else this lot did they weren't into being flash. The receptionist looked at me with thinly veiled disgust. I told her that I had an appointment with Mr Philby and she lifted the phone and whispered something to someone. I sat down and waited and five minutes later the man I'd met in the bar came out of the door behind the reception and greeted me. He ushered me into a small lift and we went up to the third floor.

'We'll only keep you for an hour or so,' he said as he opened the door into a long, thin, wood-panelled room. At the end sat four middle-aged men all in almost identical grey pinstripe suits. The man from the bar pointed me to a chair in front of the desk and went to join the other four men. There was a long period of silence as we all sized each other up like dogs in a park.

'What's your name?' barked the eldest of the men.

'Well, it looks like I'm not where I think I am if you don't know that,' I replied somewhat smugly.

'What's your name?' repeated the man without a flicker of emotion.

'My name is Jazz Black, what's yours?' I countered cheekily.

'Your real name please?' continued the man.

'My real name is gone, it's my past, I'm Jazz Black now,' I said, trying to sound profound.

'Your name is Dominic Thomas Remus Joly, you were born in Beirut, Lebanon, schooled in the UK and are currently at Chalk Farm Polytechnic. You spent a year in Morocco that resulted in you spending time in prison there for drug trafficking. You speak French and Arabic and are supposed to be studying the political systems of European city states which basically means San Marino . . .'

'And the Vatican,' I interrupted.

'Well, that's debatable,' continued the man. 'You have something of a passion for all things Gothic which has led you to recently join a band called . . . Big Black Dead . . .'

'*The* Big Black Dead,' I interrupted. 'Good name, isn't it?

I thought it would be cool hearing DJs on the radio having to say the . . .'

'We're not terribly interested,' interrupted the second man along.

'We just want to check that we've got all the facts right before putting a little proposition to you,' the third man continued. 'What are your plans for when you leave university?' he asked.

'I don't really have any, to be honest,' I replied. 'I just want to do something that is kind of what I want to do, rather than having to work to get money to do what I want to do, if you see what I mean.'

'Another slacker. So you have nothing in particular in mind?' continued the second man.

'Nothing that concrete, I'd thought of going to live in Paris for a bit and I've just written a couple of good tunes so who knows what will happen on the music side,' I replied chirpily, wondering where all this was going.

'You want to go to Paris? That's good news,' said the third man. 'I'll come straight to the point if I may,' he continued. 'We are looking to employ a couple of people and keep them on a sort of financial retainer whilst allowing them to continue with their life and studies. In return, all we ask is that they be ready to receive a call from us one day asking them to do a little work for us from time to time. The fact that you are interested in going to Paris could be very useful for us. You speak French and we have a couple of things that you could do for us out there. Your unusual appearance and interests are the sort of thing we need. We are keen to diversify the type of recruit we have. Our usual Oxbridge Classics graduate tends to stand out like a sore thumb nowadays.' He leaned back and stared hard at me. 'Would you be interested in this kind of thing?'

I tried to look nonchalant and casually inquired as to how much the financial retainer might be and when did that start?

'We would pay you £500 a week and that would start from the moment you leave this room if you agree. Of course, you would never be able to tell anyone about this arrangement or this meeting, I presume that that is understood?'

I nodded rather too eagerly as I tried to work out how much that was a month and then a year. It was a fortune. Unless this was some weird freemason type joke then I had just hit the jackpot. I had to answer some more questions about various things to do with university and dates etc. and then sign what appeared to be an abbreviated version of the Official Secrets Act. Four of the men then left the room and the last one came over and gave me a card with a number written on it.

'Ring this if there are any problems or questions. Here's a bank card and PIN. The money will be deposited in there every Sunday night, do not use this account for any other purpose and never tell anyone about it or this meeting and all will be well. Is that understood?'

I nodded and grabbed the bits of paper and allowed him to show me out into the reception where I said goodbye and left the building. A hundred yards down the street I looked down at the bits of paper before screaming with excitement. I was rich, I was fairly sure that I was a secret agent and I didn't actually have to do anything. I was a sleeper. It was perfect. I loved sleeping.

The first thing that I did with the money was to put a

down payment on a Porsche. It was not very Goth but it was black. I used to drive it around a lot but always parked it in St Martin's Lane before continuing up to college by tube. Other poly students never ventured into the West End, it was way too 'bourgeois' for them. It was great not having any money worries but I soon forgot about my weird status as a 'sleeper'. The band was going well and we had a three-song demo recorded on a four-track in someone's basement. We'd gone with 'Valium Lows' and two other songs that I'd written with Britte, 'Where Have They Buried All the Bodies?' and 'The Big Bad Murder Song'. We'd sent the tape to John Peel and he'd played 'The Big Bad Murder Song' on his show and had been really complimentary about it all. To me that was it, I was a rock star.

We got a gig supporting a small band from Rochester in Kent called The Dream Cream Fountain. The girls thought they were rubbish but I quite liked them. We were booked at the Mean Fiddler in Harlesden and they had quite a following. Everyone had come up from Kent to see them so it was useful experience for us as there was going to be a good crowd. I had a meeting with the girls and persuaded them that this would be a great opportunity for us to do a biggish gig. They were a bit surly since they felt that The Fountain were not really Goths and that we were selling out. I had grown a bit sick of the whole Goth thing by then and this was about the final straw and I lost my temper.

'What the hell is Goth anyway?' I shouted at them. 'All we do is paint ourselves white and ponce about looking unhappy with everything but we never actually do anything about it, we never just have fun like everyone else.' I felt like I'd lost my mind. Was I really renouncing Goth and the whole lifestyle that I'd been so heavily involved in for almost a year? Maybe I was growing up? Maybe I needed new things? Maybe the interview with Philby and friends had changed me in some way?

Things were never to be the same with the band after that. They started to get a bit offish with me and a couple of them didn't even turn up to the rehearsal before the gig. I didn't care. I didn't need them. But I did want to do this gig. (Oaksey always claims that this was a significant moment in my life. A definite fork in the road, where I took the left not the right. The hard, not the easy. I can't really tell but I definitely felt that I was being guided by some higher force. Oaksey says that I was closing a door to pain and opening a stairway to hope but I never really understood that. I'm sure he's right.)

The night of the gig was a weird one from the off. The girls were really friendly, almost flirty, totally different from the last couple of weeks. They insisted that we go out and have a drink before the sound check and we had about four snakebites each before going back to the venue. We had about an hour to hang around in the dressing room before the gig and we just pissed about smoking fags and nattering, just like the old times. It was nice. I was really pleased that they'd come round to my way of thinking as I'd invited quite a few old friends and a lovely half-Peruvian girl that I'd met on a bus. I'd told her a little lie that I was in The Cure and that I was doing a one-off gig for fun with some friends that night. She seemed to have completely fallen for it and I intended to leave pretty soon after the gig with her and see what happened. I was in a very good mood.

Marlene came over to me and offered me a slice of apple

and I wolfed it down before running through the set list with them one more time. We were going to kick off with 'Cold Hard Slab', quite a tricky one, and I wanted to be sure that we all came in at the right time on the first chorus. The girls didn't seem to be taking it very seriously but at least they were in a good mood and I was sure that they would be cool once we were on. I had a can of cider and was about to put my gig shirt on when I started to feel very peculiar. First the telly in the dressing room started to slow down. The newsreader took ages getting every syllable out of her mouth. I could see in the edge of the long mirror in the corner of the dressing room that my leg was jumping up and down. Everything was out of time, dancing to different soundtracks. I was terrified. What was happening? The girls came back in and I could hear their voices echo around the tiny room like screams in a canyon. I could hear my name bouncing from wall to wall. The girls' laughter was piercing the very centre of my skull and rattling around my head. They picked me up and I could feel myself moving but had no sensation of effort. I could dimly see the stage and then I was on; the lights were bright, brighter than a thousand suns and I started to sweat and then fell over an amp. Lying on the floor I could see the lights in the ceiling looking like flickering stars and there, right in the middle of the whole constellation, was Arthur.

'Arthur, what are you doing here? What's happening to me? There are thousands of little animals dancing on the curtains. Am I saying anything?' I wasn't sure whether I'd actually said anything out loud or just thought about stuff but Arthur could definitely hear me.

'You are the Christ figure, you must kill the unbelievers. Nothing must stand in your way. Now is the time for the righteous to arise, do not let anything stand in your way,' screamed Arthur, his eyes all reddened with anger. He was quite scary.

At that moment I heard the opening chords of 'Cold Hard Slab' and tried to stand up in time for my vocal cue. I managed to hold the microphone stand even though it appeared to have about forty snakes wrapped around it. As the guitars crashed into the opening bars of the verse, I could hear Arthur shouting, 'Now is the time, now is the time . . .'

I awoke in hospital two days later. Apparently I had been given a slice of apple with enough LSD on it to satisfy an entire company of GIs in Vietnam. The nurse said that I had been lucky not to sustain permanent brain damage. She asked me whether I had enjoyed the concert. She hoped that it had all been worth it. I told her that I couldn't remember anything after stumbling on stage. She laughed and said that the two people who had brought me in had told her that I had stripped naked, proclaimed myself as the new Christ and had tried to kill two members of the audience with the sharpened point of a guitar that I'd smashed over the drummer. It was, by all accounts, quite a performance. There had been an A&R man from a big record company in the audience who wanted to sign me up for a solo deal.

'You'd also better take a look a this,' she laughed, throwing a copy of *Sounds* down on the bed. The cover was a photo of me. The strapline read 'Jazz Black, the new prince of darkness?' I groaned, pushed the morphine button on my intravenous and I drifted off into a deep sleep.

The solo deal never did go anywhere. I met up with the

A&R guy and played him some of my stuff but he didn't seem that interested. He was into the whole rock'n' roll suicide-type stage presence. It soon became clear to him that the night he'd seen me had been a one-off. It was a shame really but probably for the best as any more nights like that one and I'd be dead.

During my second year I started to become more and more interested in politics. Thatcher was at the peak of her powers and if students were in agreement on any one thing it was their loathing of her and the Tory government. I felt a little embarrassed about this as I had a godfather who was the Home Secretary and several of my dad's contemporaries were fairly high up in the Tory party. I decided to join the Revolutionary Socialist People's Worker's Society as it had the most members. We didn't do much. We just used to hang around a corner in the Student Union grumbling about stuff and thinking of different things to declare a strike about and close the poly down for a day. We managed this on all sorts of topics: apartheid, Aids, amnesty, Angola, Abba being played in the student bar – and that was just the A's. I can't remember a single day that we didn't manage to close the place down.

Our real bugbear, though, was the newly imposed Poll Tax. This annoyed everyone since it actually affected them directly where it hurt, in their pockets. We heard that there was an enormous demonstration planned and we all got really excited. There was nothing we liked better than a good demo. It normally meant a top day out and an opportunity to get very pissed and cop off with some dreadlocked traveller girl who would be impressed by our revolutionary credentials. As the day of the demo approached, we realised that it was going to be quite a big deal, much bigger than anything we'd been involved in before, including our all day sit-in to demand that all lectures be simultaneously translated into Welsh, Celtic and Gaelic as a nod to the diverse roots of the United Kingdom. This was going to be a totally different deal. The press were talking about over a million people and students from all over the country organising buses to get them to London.

We decided to march under a banner penned by me which proclaimed that 'The Poll Tax is Bollax'. We arrived at the meeting place near Hyde Park Corner at around midday and quickly realised that this was going to be something special. Banners about every cause imaginable stretched as far as the eye could see. It felt like an entire decade was about to explode. I wasn't really angry about anything but got completely swept up by their energy as we swept down Park Lane. The city was ours. The police had come out in enormous numbers but were totally unprepared for our anger and determination. I remember briefly standing in Trafalgar Square listening to Tony Benn before all hell broke loose. Waves of police ran at walls of protestors using crowd railings as makeshift barricades. From behind us, dreadlocked crusties stood on the big black lions and hurled bottles of piss at the police. It was a bit like the Reading Festival.

After a bit of this the police got more serious and brought in horses and tried a couple of charges at the front line of the demonstrators. That was when things got completely out of hand. Bottles and stones rained down on the police lines and things started to turn nasty, way too nasty for me. I had been hanging around at the back enjoying the moment. The air was thick with apocalyptic screams and smoke from burning tyres. I got separated from my group and suddenly felt very isolated. This was way out of my league and I knew I needed out as quickly as possible. But this was easier said than done, since the police had sealed off the whole square. People were rushing around trying to find a weak spot where they could stage a breakout. It was soon obvious that the only place to try was the stairs on the north-eastern side of the square. It was impossible for the police to put vans across there and there was only a reasonably thin line of uniforms straddling them. I followed the assembled group who charged the stairs and, after a couple of minutes of stand-off, the front row broke through and we poured out of the square up Charing Cross Road.

The crowd went ballistic. High on their escape, they started smashing everything – shop windows, cars, bus stops. Nothing was safe. I kept well back and slipped off down one of the side alleys by the Wyndham Theatre leading to St Martin's Lane, hoping to have a fag and wait for the action to pass by. Unfortunately a large group followed me. I ran away from them only to come onto St Martin's Lane right by where I'd parked my Porsche. The pursuing crowd saw the car at the same time as I did. I noticed a couple of my Revolutionary Socialist Worker comrades in the angry mob. The moment they saw the Porsche they went nuts. They grabbed some large scaffolding poles from a nearby building and surrounded the vehicle, my lovely black 911. Tarquin, one of my lot, who insisted on being called 'Cabbage', congratulated me on my discovery and handed me a large scaffolding pole. 'You found it, you get first go,' he shouted gleefully. I picked up the pole and, with every eye on me, rammed it through the small side window, trying not to scratch the leather interior.

'Come on,' I shouted, 'there's plenty more of these bastards up the road.' But my words fell on deaf ears. They started smashing my car until it was nothing but a twisted hunk of metal. Cabbage passed me a Molotov cocktail and a lighter and urged me to finish the job off. I had no choice. Everybody stood back as I lit the rag. I was about to hurl it into my pride and joy when something spooked the crowd and everyone legged it. I was left standing in front of my battered Porsche holding a lit Molotov cocktail as three Black Marias roared up beside me and what looked like the entire riot squad jumped out. It was a fair cop.

It took a lot of explaining and a call to my godfather in the Home Office before things were finally sorted out. I really just wanted to go home but they insisted that I stay in custody for a respectable amount of time and so I spent eight hours at Her Majesty's pleasure for vandalising my own Porsche. How the police laughed.

It did increase my cred at poly. I was the only one from my group to be arrested and was instantly granted official revolutionary status. So much so that one of my 'comrades' put up a large picture of me, Molotov in hand, facing down a wall of police. They'd got it from the *Daily Star*. As soon as the poly authorities saw it, I was history. I got called in to see the principal, an earnest man whom I'd never even set eyes on before. He told me that he had little choice but to expel me. I told him about how I wasn't really involved in all that and about Philby and my godfather and that there had been no harm done as it was actually my own Porsche. He just looked at me with such pity that even I realised that this all sounded ridiculous and I gave in. That afternoon I left the poly for the very last time. My education had come to an end. I was now ready for the real thing, ready for life.

Gay Paris

I STEPPED OFF THE train at the Gare du Nord at eleven fifteen in the morning. I had nowhere to stay, nothing planned and I was happy for the first time I could remember. I had left my politics in the cells of Charing Cross police station. I was a new man in a new city looking for a new life. Philby had been very happy that I was off to Paris and my money was still coming in.

I had told everyone I knew that I was going to Paris to write my novel. Who knew, maybe I'd finally meet the lovely girl that I'd dreamed about last time I was here when I was hallucinating on magic mushrooms.

I got a studio in the Rue de Lappe – number seven, just down from a nightclub called Le Balajo. Rue de Lappe was very cool. It was just off the Place de la Bastille and minutes from the trendy Marais district. The whole Left Bank scene that so many people identified with Paris was old hat. The eleventh arrondissement was where it was at and I was slap bang in the heart of it. I spent most of my time in the bar with no name at the bottom of the street. The bar with no name was not the bar's name. The place genuinely didn't have a name and was thus known as the bar with no name. The problem was that people actually thought that that was its name and it wasn't. It was all very Parisian.

I started to grow a little goatee and developed a taste for

Pernod. For hours every day I would sit in the corner of the bar with no name, stroking my goatee, smoking untipped Gitanes and trying to write my novel. The only problem was that I had absolutely nothing to say. For hours I would stare at the blank page willing something to appear on it. It got quite embarrassing and in the end I copied out a couple of pages of E. M. Forster so that I at least had a couple of pages of writing to leave on top of my blank pile. I grew quite depressed and decided that being a novelist sucked. I resolved to get a job, something to fill the day, something that might give me the inspiration that was clearly lacking.

There was only one job that I wanted in Paris and that was to work on the *International Herald Tribune*. It sounded good, it was what the girl in *A bout de souffle* worked on and being a journalist was exactly the sort of thing that a budding novelist should have on his CV. The first problem was that the paper was not actually based in central Paris. It was miles away on the outskirts in a soulless modern development called La Cité, not unlike Canary Wharf. The second, rather more important problem was that they didn't have any jobs. Even if they did, the scary personnel woman told me, they were very unlikely to hire me as I didn't have a degree.

I took the train back to town trying hard not to be disheartened. While waiting in the reception area I had managed to pinch a large pile of *International Herald Tribune* business cards. An hour later I left a photocopy shop as the new investigative reporter for the paper and I had the cards to prove it. To anyone that I met in Paris or to anyone that came out to visit me I was working as a reporter on the paper whilst writing my first existentialist novel.

I was bored stupid. I didn't know anyone in the city and

spent most of my days wandering along the banks of the Seine trying to look moody by kicking piles of dead leaves and hoping that my mushroom dream girl would notice me and offer me a ride on her bicycle. But she never came.

About a month later I got a job. It wasn't exactly the ideal bohemian occupation but it was a start. I was a waiter in the Chicago Pizza Pie Factory just off the Champs Elysées. Because I spoke French I was the only waiter amongst forty Danish waitresses. This wasn't too bad. Chicago Pizza Pie Factory was an extraordinary place. For visiting Americans it was a temple of refuge, somewhere where they could hide away from the terror of snails and garlic and rude Frenchmen and sink their fat arses into an oversized bench and eat a mountain of doughy pizza. For the French it was an excuse to come in and have all their prejudices about foreign food confirmed. They would howl with laughter when the enormous slices of tasteless dough would land on their tables and scoff loudly at the oversized alien monsters draped in Burberry that surrounded them.

I would start the day laying the tables. This was OK as no one really bothered me. Then, as people came in, the mood changed. There was a very strict hierarchy in the restaurant. Danish women and occasional French speakers like myself were waiters. American kids who didn't speak French were the bus-boys. Moroccans made the pizzas and Portuguese women were the cleaners. There didn't seem to be any place for the French here – not that any of them ever applied.

I got to know some of the Danish girls really well. They were cool, very laid back and lots of fun. Some of them even knew some French people. One, Astrid, shared a flat with two French girls who did something in fashion. They were sweet and I started spending a lot of time round there. I did the old *International Herald Tribune* number and told them that I was writing an investigative piece on the foreign job market in Paris and was working deep undercover at Chicago Pizza Pie. I then told them about my novel and they both seemed very impressed. What was it about? the prettiest of the two asked. I told her that if I told her then I would have to kill her. She giggled and I started to enjoy Paris.

The girl's name was Claudine and she was twenty-four, a year older than me. She was a Parisian through and through. I took her out on a date in the Marais and we ate steak and drank wine and then wandered down the banks of the Seine and sat right on the point of the Ile de la Cité and watched the lights twinkle on the bridges. I could even hear an accordion playing somewhere on the other bank. It was so filmic I couldn't believe that it was happening for real. I longed to ask her if she had a bicycle – it was becoming an obsession. She asked me to recite her something from my novel and I flustered around before remembering something from Orwell's *Down and Out in Paris and London*. I struggled to remember the exact story but some bollocks about kitchen porters and tramps saw me through. I managed to get a pretty good bit of story out and I could see that she was impressed. 'I haven't really finalised anything yet, I'm just riffing around trying to get a storyline,' I said nonchalantly.

'I fink eet ees fantastique, eet ees like poetry,' she whispered over the sound of the river lapping onto our little bank.

'Do you have a bicycle?' I asked her, almost breathless

'A bicycle, *non, pourquoi*? I 'ave a Deux Chevaux, a car.'

A car, she had a car – this got even better. We could go

on long trips to Provence with a picnic and a bottle of local red wine given to us by a friendly local farmer. We would eat the picnic off the bonnet of the Deux Chevaux before wandering off into the nearby woods to drink the wine and make love on a soft bed of lavender.

'I would love for you to meet Biff,' she said eagerly.

'Biff?' I replied, slightly puzzled.

'*Mon amour* Biff, ee is an American and a poet like you, ee comes back from skiing in Colorado in two days and I fink that you two would get on really well. Ee is a journalist with *Le Monde* and ee knows lots of people at the *Tribune*. We will get together for dinner on Thursday. First I must 'ave him for me on Wednesday. I am so 'orny for heem. We will all be such good friends.'

I pretended that I needed to have a pee, got up and, the moment that I was behind a bush, I legged it. Fuck, I hated Paris.

Back at the Chicago Pizza Pie things were hotting up. I arrived there one day to find a notice pinned up on the staff noticeboard announcing that we were to host a major film-premiere party. Did anyone wish to volunteer to work at the party as waiters? I was there like a shot. This was my big break. I could schmooze the crew and cast and get myself onto a film set even if they paid me nothing. I'd soon be off doing the kind of stuff that I was clearly destined for. I knew that there had been a reason for me to work in pizza.

The following Thursday I got to work very early to get all spruced up for the big do. The restaurant had indeed been snazzed up and was looking almost welcoming.

The idea was that we set out the pizza canapés and the drinks and then the cast, crew and guests would come straight from the premiere on the Champs Elysées into our culinary paradise deep beneath Rue de Berri.

At ten o'clock sharp guests started pouring in. I still didn't know what the film was and didn't immediately recognise anyone famous. Maybe these were the hangers-on, I thought to myself. The real stars wouldn't arrive until later to make more of a splash. Sure enough, about half an hour later I heard a commotion at the front desk and could see the strobing flash of cameras just outside the front door. I grabbed a tray of drinks and muscled my way to the front of the throng just in time to see the stars of the film stride down the stairs. Now, I've never actually seen a Mutant Ninja Turtles movie and I hope I never have to but I recognised the fuckers immediately. The four turtles wandered in, in full costume, grabbed drinks off me with a patronising 'Thanks, bud' and plunged into the applauding crowd. Apparently their latest opus had been '*un succès fou*' with the Parisian public and it was pizza, pizza, pizza all round. In retrospect I don't know who I expected to wander into the place for a film-premiere party – it wasn't exactly the most glamorous celeb hot-spot in the city. Still, hope springs eternal.

We were rewarded at the end of the evening with the chance to have our picture taken with the four turtles squatting in front of us. The photograph still hangs above the front entrance of No 8 Rue de Berri. Go see it if you don't believe me.

As I left for home that night I had to step over Michelangelo, one of the turtles. He was lying on top of Astrid with one hand up her jumper and the other lost between her legs. At least someone had enjoyed themselves.

I just didn't turn up again after that. I wonder if anyone noticed.

It was ridiculous. I was in Paris with a fairly decent

income but absolutely no direction and, apart from the kicking piles of leaves thing, nothing to fill the days with.

I got another job. Again, not quite what I had envisaged when I first arrived, but I was so bored that almost anything would do. I was to spend eight hours a day in the call centre of Spatiale Cuisines, cold-calling people from torn-out pages of the Paris phone book. I had to persuade people to agree to a visit from one of the company's 'engineers' who would give them a free quote for a new kitchen. I think it was pretty clear that once the 'engineer' was in their house he wouldn't leave without 'engineering' a signed purchase order. It was hard sell and I was the door key.

Despite the company's slogan that over eighty per cent of women at any one time were considering having a new kitchen, my calls were never much welcomed. The only people who did give you the time of day were lonely old ladies who thought that you were their 'Jean-Jacques' returned to them from the Somme. To be honest you could have persuaded these women to give you their bank account numbers in about thirty seconds and God knows what would have happened if the 'engineer' ever got there. I would keep talking to them for a bit and then bid farewell before a supervisor passed behind you and smelled a 'kill'. It was soul-destroying. I left after three weeks. At least at the Pizza Factory you could hit back if someone pissed you off. No one could ever finish their pizzas and so we used to offer a doggy bag service. We had discovered that the pizzas had an almost endless capacity to absorb Tabasco. Anyone who gave us any trouble would receive a killer dose of Tabascoed pizza guaranteed to take their lips off when they waddled over to their hotel fridge for the four o'clock munchies. I was getting desperate now and wondered whether Philby would ever come up with something for me to do. I longed for something to fill my time with. I rang his number and after a couple of Mugwuffins was through to the man himself. I explained my situation and asked him whether there might be anything going that I could help him out with. He ummed and ahhed for a bit and then told me to sit tight as he'd ring me right back. He didn't and I spent three long days hanging around my studio staring at the phone.

I didn't even have a TV to while away the time. Not that I'd watch French TV anyway – it was much like Armenian TV, forty or so men and women sitting in armchairs shouting at each other until a topless woman came in and pulled a number out of a transparent ball. Then there'd be loads of confetti and cheering before the forty people started shouting again.

Finally the telephone rang. It was someone from Spatiale Cuisines just calling to find out whether I was thinking of getting a new kitchen as they could send an 'engineer' round for a free quote.

In despair I wandered down to the Violon Dingue near the Sorbonne to indulge in their happy hour. For four francs you got a Long Island iced tea that was one hundred per cent alcohol and pretty much all that you needed for a night. The Violon was a regular meeting place for foreigners in Paris. It had its own softball team and a noticeboard with flatshares on it. Everyone there would like to prove their Frenchness by explaining the play on words that made up the name of the place. Names of places were really important in Paris for some reason. The bar's actual name, le Violon Dingue, literally meant 'the crazy violin' but it was actually a play on words involving the artist Ingres and his magic violin. The idea became increasingly confused as it was passed on from Biff to Bill to Chuck. It was always amusing to hear the latest version of what the name meant as people sank into their second Long Island iced tea. I staggered back to my studio and was just shutting the front door when I heard the phone ring. I picked it up; 'Mugwuffin?' said a voice.

'I don't want a fucking kitchen,' I slurred as the full effects of the Long Island iced tea took hold.

'Mugwuffin, this is Philby,' repeated the voice in a slightly irritated fashion.

'Listen, why don't you fuck off and stick your kitchen up your arse, I'm a fucking novelist, what do I want with a fucking kitchen, I'm a cooker of words not fucking insects like you lot . . .' I think I passed out at that point as I woke up on the floor with the phone on my head and an unbelievable headache. I dimly recalled what I'd done. My only chance and I'd gone and fucked it up. I had to ring him back.

'It's Mugwuffin, I'm really sorry, I got mugged and they hit me on the head really hard, there were three of them and I managed to get two of them but I think I must have been concussed, did I speak to you last night?'

There was a long silence on the other end as Philby thought about stuff. Finally he said, 'Meet me at the Café de Flore, seven o'clock sharp. And be sober.' The phone clicked and there was a beeping sound followed by what sounded like another phone being put down but I was too hung over to care and fell into bed.

At a quarter to seven I walked out of Saint-Michel metro

station and headed up past the big fountain towards the Café de Flore. I picked up a chicken sandwich from Elias, a Lebanese guy who had a fantastic little takeaway tucked in behind the square. He asked me how my novel was going and I told him that I was halfway through and that the action had moved to Paris and he was one of the main protagonists. He beamed and waved me away as I proffered some money. I thanked him and walked out – it always worked. People love the idea of being literary heroes.

I got to the café dead on seven o'clock, sat down in the back row of the three outside rows of tables facing the street and ordered a beer. The French understand the concept of public meeting places. Unless you're in the first throes of passion you need distractions. Rather than face each other and risk hours of embarrassed silences and forced conversations the French all look outwards and people-watch. Passing traffic gives you something to concentrate on whilst, at the same time, providing an endless topic of conversation – from bad fashion to ugly pets. It's a lifesaver and that, along with the unwritten French understanding about mistresses, is why the French divorce rate is significantly lower than anywhere else. They might be annoying but they get some things right.

At ten past seven I saw Philby walk into the café. Moments later he came out again, spotted me and sat down next to me. I gestured to the waiter and he ordered an Americano and a citron pressé; I got another beer. Philby looked thinner than the last time that I'd seen him. He was looking at me curiously.

'Nearly didn't recognise you without all the Goth get-up on. Paris cheered you up, has it?' He laughed at his own joke and took a swig of his Americano.

'I'm over all that, I'm writing a novel at the moment,' I replied.

'What's it about?' he asked.

'I could tell you but I'd have to kill you,' I giggled.

'Don't fuck with me, Joly, you've had an easy ride so far but things are changing soon and we're going to need you to keep a low profile until you get the call,' he snapped.

'Oh, all right then, I'll notify the Booker Prize to take my name off the shortlist,' I said sulkily as I took a swig of beer.

'We need you back in the UK for something in a couple of months but we need to get you some qualifications; I hear that you dropped out of poly. That wasn't the smartest move,' he said, looking me straight in the eye.

'I didn't drop out, I got kicked out for the Poll Tax thing,' I replied.

'Oh yeah, you wrecked your own Porsche. You were lucky that no one actually believed that story in the office otherwise you'd have got your marching orders from us as well. I know that you were supposed to be blending in but there is a limit. We didn't actually want you to lead a bloody revolution.' He chuckled and his mood visibly lightened. 'Anyway, we need to get you into something in the UK and for that you're going to need to get an instant degree and a crash course in journalism to give you some experience. Where do you fancy graduating from? Will the Sorbonne be all right?' He grinned at my bemusement. 'I thought it might be. You graduated from there at the end of last year in Politics and International Relations. You got a first, well done.' He handed me over a brown envelope with a degree certificate in it from the Sorbonne. I sat open-mouthed. 'If anyone has any questions then tell them to ring

Pierre Videau, he's the senior tutor there and knows all about this.' He handed me a card with the name Pierre Videau on it and a number and address at the Sorbonne.

'This is amazing,' I stammered, 'thanks a lot.'

'Now,' he continued, 'as for your journalistic experience, I've arranged for you to have a two-month internship at the *International Herald Tribune*, ever heard of it?' I started laughing uncontrollably and eventually managed to ask him whether he knew any book publishers whilst he was about it. He scowled but was clearly pleased with my reaction to his connections.

'You start tomorrow, just turn up and ask for Madame Deubel.' I secretly hoped that this wasn't the woman who had dismissed me out of hand just four months previously for not having any sort of degree. I figured if it was then I could phone Philby and he would sort it out – there seemed very little that he couldn't do.

I turned to ask him what the job in the UK was but he had gone, slipped away into the Parisian dusk. I was alone, sitting at the Café de Flore, with a first-class degree from the Sorbonne, an internship at the *International Herald Tribune* and a mysterious posting in the UK in a couple of months. Lady Luck had clearly decided to come up and slap me with one of her lucky kippers. I was on a roll and I decided that, seeing as how I'd had a couple of beers, I'd ring Claudine and take my chances with Biff.

Claudine was in and, it appeared, Biff very much out. I apologised for disappearing the last time that we had met. I said that I had gone for a leak behind a bush and had slipped, knocking myself unconscious and must have fallen into the Seine. I woke up about five miles downstream with my face kept out of the water by a piece of driftwood. I had completely lost my memory and was taken in by a family of gypsies who nursed me back to health. I eventually regained my memory with the help of their age-old remedies and haunting music. I left my new-found gypsy family and made my way back to civilisation where the first thing that I'd thought about was her so here I was, saying hello again.

Would she like to help me celebrate my return from exile and re-starting my internship at the *International Herald Tribune* and would she like to have dinner with me that evening? She fell for it hook line and sinker – life couldn't get much better.

I met her in La Palette, one of my favourite bars on the Left Bank. We sat outside chatting, drinking a lovely bottle of Nuits St Georges and smoking Gitanes. I was almost delirious. She looked stunning in a pair of pedal-pushers and a figure-hugging T-shirt with the words '100% à vendre' on it. I wasn't sure if she'd nicked it from a sale in a shop or if it was very trendy, but didn't want to blow the moment by asking. There was a full moon gleaming over the dome of the Sorbonne. As we wandered arm in arm down towards Austerlitz I spotted a row of bicycles locked to a rack. I used my penknife to slip open the lock of a large black bicycle that wasn't even attached to a rack. I told Claudine to hop on but she looked nervous. I told her that we were only a hundred yards from the Rue Mouffetard and that this had been a weird dream for me for quite some time. She looked confused but followed me as I wheeled the bike to the top of the Rue Mouffetard.

Where did my obsession with this road begin? Probably in some film with Jean-Paul Belmondo where he was walking down it, the epitome of Gallic cool. It was a windy little road running down the hill from near the Sorbonne towards the thirteenth arrondissement. It normally had a fruit market on it but on closer inspection was quite naff, with loads of cheap Greek restaurants and dodgy bars. At this time of night it was almost deserted and looked quite desolate. But it was my dream, my Parisian moment and it was about to be mine.

I made Claudine sit on the handlebars like they did in the films and we started off down the road. I had never actually ridden a bike with someone on the handlebars before and it was a lot trickier than I had expected. Plus, the brakes didn't work. We started to pick up quite a speed and Claudine started to shout at me, begging me to slow down. I managed to miss the first empty market stall but in doing so threw us right into the path of a second, even larger one. Time stood still for a second as, in the moment before impact, everything became religiously clear. Claudine had stopped shouting and was rigid with anticipation. I could make out a rather erotic bead of sweat running down the nape of her neck. I felt the front wheel connect with the base of the stall and we both took off. Claudine hit first. The whole left side of her body slammed into a shop window which smashed, allowing her to be propelled even further forward onto the marble slab that normally held a splendid display of fresh fish. It looked like a mortuary slab with her bloodied body lying motionless on it. God, I was morbid! A hangover from my years as a Goth, I suppose. Then I hit. I missed the window but went hard into a wooden side-panel and I could feel the crack in my arm and I knew I'd broken it immediately.

For a while there was total silence apart from the bells. I thought that they were in my head but I soon realised that it was the alarm going off in the shop. I got to my feet and looked around me. The bike was crumpled further down the street along with the remains of the market stall. Claudine was lying supine just inside the shop window underneath a sign advertising fresh langoustines. There was glass everywhere and lights were starting to come on in the surrounding blocks of flats. I had only moments to decide what to do. I ran away.

I had broken my arm quite badly and had to spend a couple of hours in hospital having a cast put on. I got out just in time to rush back to my flat, get changed and then hop on the metro to go to the *International Herald Tribune*. I got there fifteen minutes late, which wasn't a good start. I ran up to the receptionist and told her that I was late for an appointment with Madame Deubel. As we walked down the long red corridor my heart started to sink. We were heading for exactly the same office as the one that I had been fobbed off in some months before. Sure enough, we stopped outside the large corner office and, after a knock, we entered Madame Deubel's office. She was a formidable figure, perfectly coiffed, dressed in a black-and-white Chanel suit and large, brown-rimmed glasses that made her look a little like Olga Krebss, the woman in *From Russia With Love* with the spikes coming out of her shoes. She was wearing long, thin stilettos that looked as though they might have seen similar action in their time. She regarded me with a quite breathtaking level of disgust.

'I don't know who your contacts are, but it appears that they have a certain amount of clout and I'm forced to accept you as an intern for a couple of months. I am not, however, forced to treat you nicely so don't expect any favours from me. Go and report to Alain Bovary on the fourteenth floor and behave yourself. There are about fifty people whom you've just queue-jumped and I won't hesitate in flinging you back where you came from.' She stood up, indicating that my audience was at an end.

'Thank you, Madame Deubel, I am really grateful . . .'

'Have we not met before?' she interrupted, looking over the top of her scary glasses. 'You look familiar.'

'People often say that I bear a passing resemblance to Alain Delon,' I replied pathetically.

'You look like Alain Delon?' she snorted. 'I know Alain and, believe me, you do not bear the faintest likeness to him. Now go on, get out of here and do some work.' She turned to look out her window and I was gone. I'd got away with it, just.

Alain Bovary was in his mid-forties, gay and not in the slightest bit interested in his new protégé. 'I was only told about you this morning and I really have no need for an intern. Just keep out of my way and I'll think of something for you to do at some stage. Here, read my clippings file.' He chucked me a brown leather folder bulging with various newspaper articles either written by Alain or featuring him as their subject.

Alain was clearly something of a socialite. There were pictures of him with Elton John, Grace Jones and Gianni Versace. He wrote the Parisian social column and was able to fill most of it with stories of his own exploits. This could be more fun than I had thought.

'What happened to your arm?' Alain asked, looking up from his computer at my cast.

'Oh, I was in a bike accident,' I replied quickly.

'A bike accident . . .' Alain looked intrigued.

'Yes, I'm thinking of entering the Tour de France this year and so I train at night,' I lied.

'You are going to enter the Tour de France? Do you have any experience for this?' he laughed.

'No, not really but I figure that you've got to start somewhere and when in Rome . . .'

'We are in *Paris*, my friend,' he said, looking a mite confused.

'No, no. It's an English expression; it just means that you should have a go at things.'

Alain laughed and got up from his desk and came over to me. He looked me straight in the eyes. 'Are you gay?' he said teasingly.

'No, I've got a girlfriend,' I replied nervously.

'Well, as you English say, "When in Paris . . ."' He roared with laughter before I could say anything and slapped me on the knee.

'I don't know whether you're a liar or an idiot but I like you, English boy. What do you want to learn while you are here?'

'I just want to be a journalist of some form. I'm writing a novel and I think that the experience will be very good for me and I want to learn more about life, love, everything.' I sounded like a total twat.

'OK, you will come with me, keep your mouth shut and your eyes open. You will see how a real *journaliste* does his work. Go home and come back here at seven o'clock this evening.'

'But I just got here,' I protested.

'For a social *journaliste* there is nothing to do until the sun sets – then the rats and the stories come out and dance in front of us, begging to be noticed.'

I nodded and picked up my coat; it had been the best day's work of my life so far and I wasn't complaining.

I spent the day loafing around the Marais. I went down the Rue des Rosiers and got myself an enormous falafel and sat in the courtyard of the Musée Picasso watching the tour groups wander by, flocking like sheep behind weird old men waving umbrellas above them to guide their followers.

For the next four or five weeks I had the time of my life. Alain knew everyone there was to know in the French capital. I shadowed him all round town – to premieres, theatres, book signings and intimate intellectual soirées. It soon became clear that Alain's journalistic career was a little hobby he'd acquired along the way. His problem was not finding the right story but working out what he could put in without pissing too many people off. Everyone knew what he did but he had a certain charm, a roguishness that won people over. No one ever questioned my presence. Alain was my passe-partout and we got along famously. He lived in an amazing apartment overlooking the Gare de Lyon with a huge roof terrace that looked down to the Seine. Most evenings would end up there with an extraordinary mix of people drinking chilled rosé and dancing to Gainsbourg. This was the Paris I had only read about and I was slap bang in the middle of it thanks to Philby and Alain. Strange days.

Strange days indeed, I thought, recalling Jim Morrison who had met his watery end in a bathtub just five hundred yards from Alain's flat in Rue Beautreillis. One night we even managed to blag our way into the actual flat he died in. We had read about Jim's last bar crawl in some magazine and decided to match it drink for drink. Five hours and twenty-six drinks later we ended up, obliterated, ringing the doorbell. A sleepy voice answered the intercom. We announced that we were from the Sûreté and that we had a warrant to search his flat. The door opened and we stumbled up to the second floor, trying to stifle our drunken giggles. A bleary-eyed, nervous-looking man opened his door for us and we flashed our metro passes at him and marched into the flat demanding to see the bathroom. He didn't know what was going on. We barged into the bathroom where a woman was immersed in bubbles in the very bath Jim had died in. We spent thirty seconds looking officious as she stared at us in utter horror. We excused ourselves, told the man at the door that we had been given the wrong information and legged it down the street, howling with laughter. Needless to say, this never made the paper.

Alain and I were getting on better and better and I longed to tell him about my weird Philby connection and how I'd come to get the job. I was sure he would love the whole story and would probably have an idea what it was all about. I never quite got round to it. Paris Fashion Week came round and we were launched into a series of endless defilés, drinks, and private parties in an attempt to cram as much into one debauched week as possible. Alain was in his element. His on-off boyfriend Zoltan, a Hungarian hat designer, had gone to Budapest for two weeks and so he was on his very worst behaviour. We zoomed around Paris in his Renault Four, sniffing Amyl Nitrate off the steering wheel as we bounced from party to party. The penultimate night of Fashion Week saw us starting off with an amazing show under the glass pyramid in the courtyard of the Louvre followed by a drinks party on a private *bateau mouche* moored off the Place de la Concorde before some new young designer's party at Le Casbah, a fantastically trendy night spot behind the new Opera House. We got to the Casbah at about one o'clock in the morning and the party was well underway. We went straight to the front of the queue and Alain got us in. Once inside, the air was thick with heavy smoke from two enormous incense burners. It smelled of cedar and for a moment I was taken right back to Beirut, kids firing at Israeli jets, Uday, sweet sweet Uday, roaring round Ashrafieh in a jeep, the dull thud of mortars landing in the garden and Arthur . . . I hadn't heard from Arthur for a while but there he was, clear as day.

'Hanging around with poofs now, are we? Little nancy boy, are we? Think that's all right now we're living with the French? What the hell are you doing? Gone native, have we? Hanging out with nonces? Oh we're all so chi-chi now. Maybe you don't have time for Arthur any more. Maybe we think that we're better than that, maybe the poofs know better than Arthur.' I staggered forwards, blinking rapidly, trying to get the bloody dog out of my head. This really wasn't the moment. It always went pear-shaped when he turned up and I was having too good a time.

I could still see his gurning chops right in front of me and I lashed out, trying to physically rip him out of the air in front of me. Unfortunately I only managed to knock over one of the enormous incense burners. Hot perfumed cinders went flying all over the packed room, sending models and stylists into a blind panic. One large block of molten cedar-wood soared high into the rafters of what used to be a Turkish bathhouse before falling back to earth on the lap of a rather fragile-looking girl sitting in a wheelchair. She seemed to be quite heavily sedated as she reacted very slowly to the fact that the silk pashmina trendily covering her legs had burst into flames. She screamed as the flames started licking up her dress and managed to turn the wheelchair round to face me. It was at this moment that I realised it was Claudine. I grabbed the handles of the wheelchair and turned her round a full one hundred and eighty degrees. She looked up in blind panic and our eyes met. Her mouth fell open but I don't know if it was the pain of the fire or the shock of seeing me again. I didn't hang around to find out. I mumbled my apologies before giving her wheelchair a firm push, propelling it fast across the room so that it turned into something akin to an Ancient Greek siege machine. The wheelchair's wheels hit the edge of the large ornate fountain that formed the centrepiece of the room and, for the second time in under five weeks, Claudine found herself airborne. For one glorious second she was a golden comet shooting through the room on her own very special trajectory. The next second she hit the water and steam rose from the fountain as she sank beneath the tiny waves. Several people finally abandoned their Vogueish poses of disbelief and plunged in to recover the now inert charred body floating in the middle of the fountain. I decided that this might be an opportune moment to call it a night.

Claudine lived. I know this because there was quite a lot of press about the incident in the Casbah and she was able to give the police a garbled statement before lapsing into a coma. The doctors said that she was severely traumatised but would probably pull through in the end. The papers said that she had talked of a young Englishman who had courted her and had subsequently made two attempts on her life. She knew very little about him but what details she did give made my staying in Paris pretty risky.

I rang Philby and filled him in a little, leaving out the gory details and told him that I would have to return to England early. He didn't seem too annoyed and told me to get in touch once I was back and settled. I promised him that I would. I rang up Alain and told him that I had to go back to England as I had been called up to serve in the Gurkha regiment and was off to Hong Kong a week tomorrow. It was a really crap lie and I realised that I was bordering on the pathological. Alain didn't believe a word of it, I knew that. He didn't say anything though. He wished me luck and hoped that I'd come back to see him one day. I promised him I would. I packed my bags, locked my studio for the last time and headed off to the train station. It was time to start my life proper, again.

Last Night I Dreamt of Mandy

I WAS ACTUALLY QUITE glad to be back in the UK. Things had really changed. A couple of friends had got decent jobs and everyone seemed to be in a better mood. Thatcher had gone and her tear-stained departure from Downing Street seemed to have really cheered everyone up. The new Prime Minister, John Major, was perfect. No one was ever going to compete with Thatcher and so electing a dull grey bank manager was an inspired idea. No one thought that he would last very long but all were enjoying the joke while it lasted. Little did I know that our paths would soon cross in such a curious manner. I moved into a house with two people that I knew from school just off Earls Court Road. I wouldn't exactly describe them as friends but at least they hadn't written nasty graffiti about me in the school loo so it was a start.

I was keen to know what Philby had in mind for me but didn't want to look too uncool by ringing him immediately. One of my flatmates was making some serious cash by doing charcoal portraits of tourists on Kensington High Street. He was clearing about £200 a day with a very relaxed schedule. This sounded brilliant so, ignoring the fact that I really couldn't draw, I got myself a flip-pad, easel and some thick pencils and set off for Holland Park. I decided to give myself a little helping hand. Using some tracing paper, I drew the outline of both a man's and a woman's face and filled in most of the details. Then I simply had a pile of these hidden behind a blank sheet of paper. When the subject sat down I flipped over to the correct profile and then tried to fill in a couple of details that would personalise it like curly hair or a big nose. Admittedly the portraits looked not unlike potatoes but I'd never claimed to be an artist and these idiots were just doing it because they were bored anyway. What were they expecting, a van Gogh?

The day went by all right – there was a lot of grumbling but no one actually managed to get their money back and by lunchtime I had made £50. Unfortunately I hadn't realised that the pitches for portrait artists were a bit like ice-cream vans. They were jealously guarded by a vicious bunch of thugs who didn't take kindly to someone muscling in on their turf. Just after lunch a large Arab-looking man approached me and told me in no uncertain terms that I should fuck off. I refused and he wandered off, leaving me to assume that my unspoken inner violence had won the day. Half an hour later he was back with three friends who dragged my easel and me into some bushes just by the youth hostel and gave me an extraordinarily thorough kicking. They were Iraqis and clearly felt very strongly about being the only artists in that particular area. In between kicks to the head I managed to drop my old friend Uday's name in the hope that this might ring a bell. If anything, it seemed to turn them into vicious psychopaths. They started to get so violent that I wondered whether I was going to survive the beating. Lesson one: never drop old school friends' names without knowing what they are up to. He was clearly as popular in Baghdad as I was in London.

When they finally finished I limped out of the park never to return.

I rang Philby the next day and we agreed to meet at a pub called the Windsor Castle on the crest of Campden Hill near Notting Hill. We sat in the garden at the rear and drank pints of cold cider. It was a balmy London summer evening and the place was packed.

'What the fuck happened to your face?' he blurted out straight away.

'I got into a misunderstanding with some Iraqis,' I replied.

'You really are a fucking idiot,' he said, trying to sound disapproving, but I got the feeling that he actually thought better of me for it. We exchanged a little bit of banter before he came to the point. 'I have a job for you. It's a good one, very interesting and very important to us. It's as an intern with one of the TV news groups at Westminster. You'll be working on all sorts of political stuff and you'll get a feel for TV as a bonus.'

I was overjoyed. I'd loved the idea of working in TV but didn't have a clue how to do it and here it was being offered to me on a plate. Everyone should have a Philby, I thought. 'What is it you actually want me to do for you?' I asked, trying to sound professional but not really caring.

'I want you to try and keep an eye out for the new breed of Young Labour supporters. Try and make friends with them, join a couple of organisations, just keep us informed about what's going on.'

'How am I going to know what you're after? Is it Reds under the beds kind of stuff?'

'No, that's all old hat, we're after the new smoothies. We've got moles in holes all over the old left and we don't have enough room to store all the stuff we've got on the Tories. We need some dirt on the new lot.' He smiled as he said the word dirt. I knew that he was after a little more than dodgy manifesto promises. This could actually be quite fun. I shook Philby's hand as we said goodbye. He held onto it just a fraction longer than necessary. 'Don't let me down. I've got faith in you but others don't.' He winked and disappeared into the crowd by the door of the beer garden.

The next Monday I turned up at a building on Millbank to start my new career in TV journalism in a Nicole Farhi suit that I'd bought after lusting after it for a couple of weeks. It was a thin brown pinstripe, smart with just a hint of cool. Very New Labour, I thought to myself. I was also breaking my dad's primal rule of not wearing brown in town. It felt good. I slotted into my new job quite quickly. Although my journalistic credentials were bogus, I did have a basic interest in politics and especially in the internal machinations and gossip of the Westminster village. I was put to work on a relatively unwatched midday programme called *News in Parliament* that documented the workings of parliament and discussed what was coming up that afternoon. There were a couple of guests and a couple of VT stories. My job was to research the VT stories for the reporters. I had to set up interviews, find locations and generally try to make the piece as interesting and varied as possible. I would often be working on a couple for later in the week as well as polishing off one for that day's programme. As the transmission time neared each day I did tend to go to pieces. I have never worked well under pressure. (Oaksey thinks that this is because of my childhood stuff with the war. He tells me that I'm what he calls a stress buckler not a puncher.

Stress bucklers can't handle pressure, cave in easily and block stuff out. Stress punchers stand up to it and have it out there and then like a street fighter.)

The part I loathed more than anything else was having to go and grab a soundbite off a politician on Westminster Green, so we could have the background shot of Big Ben in the package – presumably to remind anyone watching what subject we were covering. It was normally for someone else's story and so I wouldn't really have followed what it was all about. I would have to get a couple of answers off the interviewee that we could edit down and insert into a bigger package. Normally it didn't matter what you asked as they only had one thing to say and they would endlessly repeat it until everyone felt that they had said it enough times. Unfortunately for me, there was the occasional politician who actually waited for a question and then answered it properly. One morning I arrived at the office a bit late only to be sent straight out onto the Green to talk to Stephen Dorrell, a Tory moderate, about something that I knew nothing of at the time and have subsequently forgotten. I arrived on the Green to see Dorrell already there, standing next to the old camera guy and his sound man who had been working there for years and were known by everyone as Dastardly and Mutley. I shook Dorrell's hand, grabbed a stick mike and tried to work out what on earth this could be about.

DJ: Mr Dorrell, what are your views on what's happened today?
SD: What do you mean, my views?
DJ: Where do you stand on this issue?

SD: Are you talking about Europe?

DJ: Yes, definitely, tell me about Europe, where do you stand on the current problem?

SD: I don't think that there is a problem but I clearly said that I wouldn't talk about this at the moment, the issue is health . . .

DJ: Are you ill?

SD: Is this some sort of joke? I was asked here to comment on Labour's statement on hospital trusts.

DJ: Can you trust them?

SD: Who?

DJ: Labour.

SD: Not on this, but is that what you mean?

DJ: So could you give me a clean soundbite saying you can't trust them on health and that should be what they want.

SD: What who want?

DJ: My editors.

SD: How long have you been doing this?

DJ: Oh ages but I have a medical condition today and my head hurts.

SD: Right, I'm going to go now if you don't mind.

DJ: OK, don't worry about the soundbite, I'll get something from what you said, it was very interesting, thank you.

I was trying my best.

It was a cool place to work. Most people were pretty bright and worked and played hard. There was a good social scene in the bars around Westminster and I started to get to know quite a few people. There were basically two definite types of people: the budding politicos who were working in news whilst they paid their dues to their party of choice. They would eventually stand for a couple of no-hoper seats and then, if everything went according to plan, get a safe seat. This section divided itself into two sub-groups. The young fogeys wore sports jackets and cords and looked as though they had just stepped out of some university common room in the 1930s. These were the young Tories and it was instantly clear by looking at them that they were on the way out. Labour youth were the very opposite; most sported little steel rectangular glasses and wore slightly shiny modern suits. They looked more like flash estate agents than enemies of the state, but these were the people that I was supposed to watch.

The other principal type of person in Westminister was the budding news star. Excessively keen and hard working, they were news obsessed and determined to make as many contacts as possible in every area of political life. They all idolised Jeremy Paxman and would have cut anyone's throat to get to his position. If I was being honest, there wasn't that much difference between them and the politicos but at least the journalists were allowed to be cynical. There was a feeling that everyone was only here for a while on their way to greater and better things. It was a very exciting place to be young.

I joined a New Labour group called Red Rose, a group that met up regularly to introduce like-minded people to the New Labour agenda. We were supposed to bring along someone new each time so that they could be given the schmooze. As it was, it tended to be an excuse for a piss-up and an attempt to snog the women or men, depending on your tastes. Most members were from PR, advertising or journalism; it was the beginning of the New Labour media stranglehold and I had no idea what I was doing in the thick of it. For the first time in my life, I was almost doing what I was supposed to be doing. It was slightly worrying.

A few senior figures in the Labour Party used to attend functions and gee up support by their presence. Peter Mandelson was the highest profile of these. He had a little gang of obsessively loyal, fanatical and smug young helpers who either worked for him in the House or at Labour HQ. I first met him at a function at King's College on the Strand. I was introduced to him by a mutual acquaintance and he asked me what I did. I told him that I was working for *News in Parliament* and his eyebrows rose almost imperceptibly. I could see that I was a potential grooming project. He moved on, gliding through the room with the ease of an ambassador's wife proffering Ferrero Rocher at a cocktail party. He left early and the room buzzed with excitement and chit-chat. I had just smelled power for the very first time.

That weekend I bumped into Mandelson in Notting Hill Gate. He was looking at jackets in a small motorcycle shop run by Laura Ashley's son – not really the kind of place I expected to see him. He appeared slightly flustered but he recognised me and invited me to join him for a coffee. We sat down at the back of a dingy coffee bar on the corner of Chepstow Road and chatted for what seemed like ages. I had never really looked at his face in detail but his manner was very attractive. He had finally shaved off the rather hideous moustache that he had been sporting. I found myself transfixed. His thin lips batted open and closed as he told me about some terrible indiscretion to do with a member of the shadow cabinet and a jockey. I laughed and his eyes twinkled. We got on well. We chatted about music. He liked Supertramp and had all their albums and we talked for what seemed like hours about 'The Logical Song'. He agreed with my theory of a masonic subtext. After the coffee we wandered through Holland Park, stopping to throw a coin into the Japanese pond of the Kyoto garden. We gazed at enormous fish swimming under the lilies. He said that he loved fish and that he really wanted some for his new London place. I laughed and said that I liked fish as well. We were both fish people, I thought to myself. Wasn't that great?

He confided in me that he was having some personal problems and that he'd really enjoyed our meeting. I'd apparently completely taken his mind off everything. I laughed and he laughed and then we shook hands and went our separate ways. I looked back just in time to see him do the same. We both looked away quickly. Something weird was going on. I skipped back home where my flatmates were having a barbecue in the garden. I was in an amazing mood and drank loads and got very pissed. I eventually retreated to my room where I gazed at a copy of the *Guardian* that had a big picture of Mandelson on the third page. That night I dreamt of masons and Mandy and slept like a log.

The next morning was a Sunday and I couldn't get Mandy out of my head. I couldn't work out whether I had suddenly become gay or whether I was simply smitten by the proximity of power. I wandered down the Portobello Road and came across an open pet shop. I acted on instinct. I purchased two red fish and carried them in a huge glass fishbowl over to Northumberland Place. I nearly bottled it. What the hell was I doing? I thought about leaving the fish on the doorstep and running away but realised that might seem a bit odd. I rang the bell and waited. Out of the corner of my eye I noticed movement in a car just opposite the house. Suddenly the door opened and Mandy stood there resplendent in a black silk kimono.

'Hello,' he said.

'Hello,' I replied. There was a long silence as we both assessed the situation.

'Won't you come in?' said Mandy, sounding like he'd made a decision.

'I've brought you some fish,' I said, holding up my enormous fishbowl.

'Thanks but I don't even have a kitchen in here yet, I've just moved in.'

'These aren't for eating, you said yesterday that you wanted fish, when we were in the Kyoto garden.'

Mandy looked confused and for a moment I wondered whether I might have made some terrible mistake. Maybe I had dreamt all of yesterday? Maybe I was having a flashback? What the hell was I doing here on this stranger's doorstep at eleven in the morning handing him a couple of red fish?

'Come in, I'm only teasing,' said Mandy, grabbing the fish and ushering me into his very spartan living room. An Eames chair and footstool sat in isolation by the back window. The effect was very modern, very arch, very New Labour.

'Do you want something to drink?' said Mandy.

'Yeah, that would be great,' I replied, starting to enjoy the moment. Mandy brought out a couple of beers and I

257899871   257899871

My great-grandfather
just after his arrest for
chloroforming penguins
in London Zoo.

Arthur,
my 'brown dog'.

Although toothy, I was a
very attractive baby.

الاسم:
الشهرة:
NOM : JOLY
اسم الأب:
Prénom: DOMINIC
اسم وشهرة الأم:
Père : JOHN ROMOLUS
الجنسية: بريطانية
Mère : Yvone
الولادة:
Nat. :
الصنعة:
Naiss.: 1967 طرابلس
الوضع العائلي:
Prof. :
رقم الوثيقة:
Fam. :
تاريخ إصدارها:
Pass. : B 91787
مكان إصدارها:
Date : 1969
العنوان: الزلقا على صايرون
Lieu : Beyrouthe
Adr. :
المستند بتاريخ
Doc.
وصابقتة

Validité de séjour jusqu'au H 4 11987

DIRECTEUR GÉNÉRAL

مديرعام الأمن العام لشؤون الأجانب

عنه
المفوض العام المتاز مصطفى العقور

١٩٨٦/٤/٨

Me at *lycée* in
Beirut 1975
(I'm second from
left – back row).

From an early age I was
a dedicated follower of
fashion (Beirut 1978).

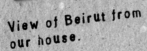

View of Beirut from
our house.

My first machine gun.

The SOUNDS front cover that heralded the musical career I turned my back on.

Costello, Spandau, Fastway, Sylvian LPs

THE RITE STUFF

SOUNDS

Bunnymen, Brilliant, SoD dates

JAZZ BLACK
THE NEW KING OF ROCK
ASSOCIATES ALEXEI SAYLE
BABIES JAMES KING
GETTING THE FEAR

Pic by Tony Mottram

Even goths need travel passes.

Valid for use only by person shown with a railcard bearing the same number.

2834C

Date of Birth 15.11.67

P.J.R. JOLY
Name of Holder

PHOTOCARD

CHALK FARM
SU PRESENTS
ZODIAC
MINDWARP
PLUS A FLOCK
OF SEAGULLS

AT THE STUDEN
UNION BAR

5TH OCTOBER
DOORS OPEN 7.30
TICKETS £2.50
FROM SU OFFICE

PLUS NIRVANA

Flyer for the big poly gig I organised. In hindsight I should have made Nirvana more prominent.

THE STUDENT UNION presents....

The Big
Black Dead

plus Special Guests

at CHALK FARM POLY
WEDNESDAY 17th
APRIL '87
8.00-12.00

Tickets £2.50 from the student union

Ticket for our band's very first gig.

My first day in Morocco –
the man in the photo
with me said he was a
dentist but I didn't
believe him.

My *carte orange* from Paris.

On my roof in Paris
doing some 'experimental'
Polaroid photography.

An invitation to lunch with the ambassador – he was an awful cook, a fact I unwisely pointed out to him.

Me and Ludmilla on Charles Bridge, Prague.

The Ambassador, Head of the Delegation of the Commission of the European Communities and Mrs Leopoldo Giunti

request the pleasure of the company of

MR Dominic Joly

for Lunch at the Residence
at 12 noon on Monday 11 January

U Laboratore 24
162 00 Praha 6

R.S.V.P
52 20 51...
CX4. 2...

Me on Charles Bridge.
Prague castle is in the background.

Me hard at work as
a diplomat for the EU.

Gorgeous Ludmilla, my other half.

Paparazzi shots
of me and
the fish outside
Mandelson's house.

My greeting card that
I love giving to my fans.

Dom Joly Comedian

This is to certify that you
met me and thought that
I was brilliant.

I liked you too.

Sometimes the tabloids speak the truth.

Don't Trust this Man

TRIGGER HAPPY TV

Move over Ali G ..here comes Dom J

JOLY IS NEW KING OF PRANKSTER TV

BY EMILY SIMPSON

SPOOF, WHOLE SPOOF AND...

Posters of this went up all over UK to promote TRIGGER HAPPY.

Evening Standard

PICK OF THE NIGHT

Trigger Happy TV
C4, 9.30pm

Reviews were kind and I used to stay up late memorising every word.

FIGHTING THE FORCES OF BOREDOM

This man is a liar 4

TRIGGER HAPPY TV
STARTS TONIGHT AT 9.30PM

I sued Channel 4 when they put this on the front page of every daily newspaper. It was only later that I realised it was an advert for the show. Brilliant.

Comedy is not always as glamorous as it seems.

Me, now. Happy and very rich.

drank mine as he went upstairs to take a phone call. When he came down five minutes later he looked like he was up to something.

'Have you ever tried absinthe?' he asked.

'Oh yeah, I love it, have you got any?' I replied, playing for time as I tried to remember what the fuck absinthe was. I knew it was some kind of strong drink that fucked up Toulouse Lautrec but I'd never had it and didn't want to show myself up.

'A friend of mine brought me a bottle back from Prague and I've developed quite a taste for it. You should be careful if you haven't had it before – it can really play tricks on you.'

'I've had it loads of times,' I said pompously.

Mandy brought in a tray carrying a green bottle, two small glasses, some sugar and a spoon. 'It's quite a ritual, they take it very seriously in Prague,' he said, flicking open a lighter under a spoon full of sugar. To be honest, I thought that things had really taken a jump into the wild side. It looked as though we were now about to launch into a serious bit of chasing the dragon, something I really wasn't prepared for. I had to say something.

'Uuhm, I don't . . . I don't do scag,' I said, trying to sound like I used to but had got bored of it.

Mandy looked at me like I was some kind of idiot. He gently explained that this was how you did it in Prague. You melted the sugar in the spoon and then stirred it into a glass with the absinthe and a bit of water. The colour was evil but I thought that it might be quite fun to try.

'What are you doing later?' asked Mandy as he stirred the absinthe.

'Nothing,' I replied, a little surprised.

'I've got a memorial lunch for some Whitehall grandee. There'll be loads of people there. Major's going and so is Kinnock. Do you want to be my date?' he asked, looking up at me coyly.

'Yeah . . . yeah, that would be cool, I'd love that,' I stammered as my mind raced at a hundred miles an hour.

I had been put into this job to learn about the New Labour movement and here I was in Peter Mandelson's home doing absinthe and about to meet the Prime Minister as his date. I wasn't doing too badly. I liked Mandy. There was a playful side to him that didn't come out in the profiles. He was eager to please but tempered this with an extraordinary aura of confidence. We clinked glasses and both downed them in one shot.

'Not many people can keep their cool with this stuff, it took me ages. Are you sure that you'll be all right?' I nodded, trying to look nonchalant whilst simultaneously dealing with the absolutely vile taste of the absinthe. Mandy excused himself to go upstairs and get changed for lunch. He chucked me down a clean shirt and tie and told me that I'd be fine in that. 'It's all pretty casual,' he shouted down. I had a fair idea that Mandy's idea of casual and mine would be a little different. He came down and switched on a large Bang & Olufsen telly in the corner.

We watched a bit of *On the Record* before we left as he had given some interview for it. He appeared pretty pleased with it but was irritated by some point John Humphrys had made after he'd gone. He picked up the phone and rang some number and gave whoever answered the phone one of the most severe tongue-lashings that I'd ever heard. The poor guy at the other end clearly didn't get a word in edge-ways. Mandy slammed the phone down. I thought that he was furious but he turned to me and burst out laughing. 'That fucker won't do that again in a hurry. Come on, let's go.' We left his house and got into a waiting Volvo. I leaned back into the tan leather back seat. I wasn't feeling too great. I could just hear Mandy tell the driver that we were off to somewhere on Birdcage Walk and I was gone. London passed by the window like little Polaroid flashes. Mandy was on the phone to someone so his chat provided the soundtrack to an absinthe-driven stumble down memory lane. There was Little Venice, the canal lapping prettily on the multi-coloured houseboats moored all the way along the banks. Down Edgware Road past Claude Agius's Vespa repair shop. There was Damon Albarn coming out of it, no doubt having had yet another vintage model re-sprayed some trendy mod colour. Down to Marble Arch past Maroush, the twenty-four-hour Lebanese restaurant where you could sit at the bar at any time of night in any state and have the best chicken sandwich this side of Beirut. On we drove down Park Lane, Mandy talking to someone about some loan for a house. He kept saying that everything would be just fine. I was feeling fine. There was the Met Bar, closed at this time of the morning but the ultimate desti-nation for London's wannabees. Some girl from Sky News Entertainment had taken me there one night. The car swept round Hyde Park Corner and turned down towards the Palace. (I'd tried to climb into the gardens one night for a bet after someone's birthday party. I was still a Goth then and I got my ankle-length leather coat caught on the last roll of barbed wire. I hung there for twenty minutes before being discovered by a passing dog patrol. I was lucky to just get a caution.)

The car turned in to the top of Birdcage Walk just opposite the Guards Museum. A large American was making stupid faces next to a guardsman as his equally corpulent wife tried to take his picture whilst keeping hold of their two rotund children. The bayonet on the guardsman's gun glistened in the sun. I felt sure that he longed to plunge it into the burger-muncher's stomach but he showed admirable restraint. As we reached the corner where the Treasury started, the car stopped and we got out. The sudden rush of air made me feel momentarily better. I followed behind Mandy. There was a lot of security about but no press. Three enormous black Jaguars sat outside, their engines purring, waiting for their occupants. Two policemen in Day-Glo jackets came to check us out and then stepped back when they recognised Mandy. We were ushered into a huge room. The atrium echoed with the noise of polite political chit-chat. Mandy soon forgot all about me as he wandered round. He really was made for this sort of event. He pressed flesh, kept moving, laughing conspiratorially, patting people on the back. He seemed to be totally unaffected by the absinthe. I, on the other hand, was just reaching the summit of what had been a very curious climb. The first half hour had made me slightly melancholic, almost nostalgic. I was now being overtaken by a truly different creature. The mix of the noise, the heat of the masses and the sudden isolation enhanced the already heady effects to something approaching full hysteria. I sat down on a solitary chair in the corner by the bar and spent ten minutes trying not to shout the word 'cunt' as loudly as I could. I wasn't even angry. I have a dim memory of John

Major coming in as a little hush rippled around the room. Not the sort of hush that you might have had if Kennedy or De Gaulle had entered. Just the sort of hush that people give when their boss walks into a room. Major was certainly no iconic figure but he was still the Prime Minister. You couldn't help being impressed.

Then things really got out of hand. People started growing heads and horns. All around me voices started to sound like birds cheeping louder and louder. No sign of Arthur, thank God. (Oaksey says that as the illness developed I started to suppress Arthur as a separate part of my consciousness. He just became another part of a single psyche. I was really glad that he wasn't there. I really didn't need a slobbering dog urging me to kill when there was so much security about.) I was convinced everyone was looking at me. I stood up and nearly fell over, steadied myself and tried to talk to the horned goat manning the bar. He looked at me and asked me whether I was all right. I made the sign of a cross with my fingers and backed away from him. He wasn't going to get me without a fight. Something tapped my shoulder and I swung round, half slapping it as I turned. It was Mandy and he had gone a very peculiar colour of orange.

'What the fuck is wrong with you, been sucking a satsuma?' I snarled as Mandy took a step back, his orange glowing face looking concerned.

'Do you want me to get the driver to take you home?' asked Mandy.

'Home? I'm fine, having a great fucking time. I've just told the fucking goat at the bar this, why am I repeating myself?' I started to exhale loudly and slowly, like a dying balloon.

'Listen. You're in no state to be here, I thought you could take your absinthe?' Mandy looked around furtively.

'What have you done with my fucking fish, you bastard,' I started to shout. 'You've killed my fucking fish, you monster, you fucked my fish.' Mandy was beating a hasty retreat and I could see two plain-clothes security men starting to wander towards me, their silver horns gleaming in the lights from the bar. This was getting out of control and I couldn't do anything about it. I turned round and dropped to all fours. I wasn't going to let these bastards take me alive. I scuttled through a group of pinstriped men and made a sharp left turn past a couple of Tory maiden aunt types. They gave me a curious look but didn't say anything and I was temporarily away. I got to a wall and stood up next to two men deep in conversation. They were both scaly, with a purple hue to the skin. They were clearly lizards, but of a type that I hadn't come across before. I thought that if I chatted to them then I might be left alone. Act normal, act normal, get a grip. I shook the first lizard by the hand and asked him what line of work he was in. I felt a surge of power that allowed me to behave normally for a second. As the lizard replied that he was in politics his lizard face split down the middle. His left-hand side looked a lot like John Major, the Prime Minister. I was stupefied. Had they got to the PM? Was I the only one who knew? Someone had to do something, act natural, bide your time.

'What do you do?' asked the Prime Minister lizard.

'I am the god of hellfire,' I replied, trying to sound casual. The Prime Minister lizard and his reptilian companion chuckled.

'I see,' said the lizard PM. 'Are you standing for election, the Lib Dems need a bit of hellfire in their campaign, maybe you could help out?' The lizard PM burst out laughing and his companion looked around at the approaching security. Their laughter echoed around my head. Now, suddenly, it all made sense. The country was being run by a lizard. No one else knew. It was like that programme *V*. They could hide it from others. The country was in peril and I was the only one who knew about it. I must act, I thought. I must act right now.

I threw the first punch before the lizard had stopped laughing. It hit him straight in the mouth and did some damage to the two large incisors that were poking out below his lip. All I knew for certain was that the PM was inside the lizard and he needed to be rescued. I grabbed the lizard's face and started trying to rip away the skin. It was strong but I managed to get a handful and start pulling. Then I was hit from behind and everything went a beautiful white. I was floating, high above my prostrate body. The lizards were going mental and being dragged down some stairs towards the light. I floated up higher into the atrium dome as the screams got louder. I could see Mandy, freeze-framed in the middle of the crowd. He was stock still in the middle of the mêlée, everyone running round him. Then everything went black.

I awoke in a strange hospital room, restrained to the bed by two cloth straps. The room had one table in it with a perfunctory bunch of flowers sitting sadly in a white shapeless vase. A television was suspended on a bracket on the wall but the plug dangled down from behind it. I had a wall light overlooking my bed but I couldn't reach the switch. The blinds on the window were shut but I could just make out the daylight behind them. Then it all came back clear as a bell. The absinthe, the lizards, the fight, the PM. Jesus Christ, had I really attacked the PM? The door to the room opened and a nurse peered in. She saw my opened eyes and closed the door again quickly. I could hear her rushing down some corridor. Five minutes later the door re-opened and two doctors came in, accompanied by a man in a suit who didn't look in any way medical.

'So, you're conscious. We need to do a couple of tests on you if you don't mind?' said the first doctor.

'Where am I?' I asked.

'You're in a hospital, you've had a traumatic experience,' said the second doctor.

'Am I under arrest?' I asked.

'No, not for the moment. It seems that you have some important friends. The press don't know where you are and no decision has been made as to what is going to happen to you,' said the man in a suit.

'I want to go home,' I pleaded.

'I think that it's going to be a long time before you go home,' said the man in the suit. 'Just calm down and someone will come and talk to you later. For the moment let these gentlemen do what they need to do.' He smiled at me.

'Yeah, fine, whatever they want, I'm just tired . . .' I could feel myself drifting off. When I woke up Philby was sitting in a chair next to my bed.

'Morning. What the hell have you gone and done now? I set you up in a cushy job and all you have to do is keep tabs on a couple of junior wannabees. Instead you end up getting pissed at Peter Mandelson's and assaulting the Prime

Minister. Top job, just what we wanted . . . not.' Philby was almost laughing.

'I wasn't pissed – it was absinthe,' I whispered.

'I have to admit that you really pulled one out of the bag this time. What am I going to do with you? Have you seen the *Standard*?' He chucked it onto my bed. I looked at the front page and groaned. The headline read 'PM Attacker in Fishy Link to Mandelson'. There was a picture of me standing at Mandy's front door proffering a fishbowl as he stood there looking splendid in his black silk kimono.

'I'm fucked, what's going to happen to me?'

'Well, it'll come as no surprise that you've been fired from TV news. I know that you've just come back but I think that you're going to have to make a little trip out of the country for a while. The PM is fine, just a little shocked, and Mandy has been trying to cover the whole thing up by claiming that you took the wrong dosage of some prescription medicine. Basically it's all a bit shaky but if the press gets hold of you you'll be fucked. Luckily for you they don't know where you are yet. I've arranged for you to take a posting as an intern in the European Commission's Delegation in Prague. You can lie low there for a while – you'll enjoy yourself. This is the last time that I'm helping you out so you'd better keep your nose clean. You leave tomorrow. Is all this clear?' Philby stared at me with threatening eyes.

'Where the fuck is Brag?' I mumbled as I drifted off into another long sleep. What else could go wrong? I was on the move again.

Czeching Out

I GROANED AUDIBLY AS the Czech Air plane landed at Prague airport. The place was a dump. Two decrepit Russian twin-rotor helicopters sat rusting away under a dimly flickering neon sign that occasionally formed the word PRAHA. It was the middle of nowhere. Dirty brown bushes lined a dirty brown road down which a dirty brown Skoda taxi rattled me towards downtown Prague. After twenty minutes of the most consistently depressing architecture and surroundings that I'd ever seen, leaving aside a drunken visit to Coventry, I was ready to turn around, go home and face the music. Communist architecture is so breathtakingly devoid of any aesthetic beauty that you almost have to admire the gall of it. As we passed yet another bunch of crumbling, soulless tower blocks I spotted the English words 'Fuck off people' scrawled in five-foot-high letters along the outside of the fifth floor of one of the blocks. It was unclear whether this was the reaction of one of the inhabitants to the world in general or simply the architect's last blast before retreating to his dacha to shoot himself in the mouth.

My surly cab driver turned round to me, completely ignoring the road, and started blabbering on in Czech, which seemed to have absolutely no root in any language that I'd ever heard before. It sounded like Klingon. He could have been telling me that we were ten minutes away from our destination or that he was going to take me to an even more desolate place, cut me up into little pieces, stuff them into a suitcase and throw it off the Charles Bridge before visiting a strip joint dressed in my clothes. I rather hoped that it was the former and nodded enthusiastically, praying that I hadn't just sealed my fate. He looked at me for a couple of seconds longer than necessary and then turned to face the road just in time to swerve out of the way of an oncoming tram. Suddenly the Skoda bumped over the crest of a nondescript-looking brown hill and there, spread out beneath me, was the old city of Prague, breathtakingly beautiful, with its golden spires glinting and windy cobbled lanes divided by a river spanned by magnificent Parisianesque bridges. I was in shock. Why had I never heard of this place? It was fucking magnificent. As the Skoda descended into Mala Strana, the riverside district on the castle side, I grew more and more excited. Gorgeous women wandered past slightly spoddy-looking men, their stilettos puncturing the thin film of snow that lay across the old city. I got out of the Skoda at my destination, a hotel called The Three Ostriches, just by the Charles Bridge, the centrepiece of the city: a cobble-stoned, pedestrianised, medieval bridge jam-packed with people crossing the river Vltava. My hotel was ludicrously cheap considering its location. Behind the hotel, high on the hill, loomed Prague Castle, dominating the city's skyline. It was from these windows that Catholics had been thrown to their deaths, giving Prague its very own speciality of execution: defenestration.

My job didn't start for a few days so I spent the time getting to know the city. Within hours I was in love. The 'Velvet Revolution' had just happened and the place was still in euphoric celebration. Night after night the citizens of Prague had convened in their hundreds of thousands in Wenceslas Square and shaken their house keys in unison in a Bohemian indication to the Communists that their time was up. It worked, and two weeks after the demonstrations had started they were free. Václav Havel, the playwright and dissident, took over the new administration and the place had been a non-stop party ever since. It was also still a McDonald's-free zone with almost zero advertising. The idealism and optimism were infectious. As the main resistance to the Communists had been intellectuals there was no real alternative political class in waiting. The government was therefore being run by a collection of playwrights, novelists, poets and musicians. Frank Zappa and Lou Reed had just been appointed honorary Cultural Attachés. For this brief moment it seemed to be the kind of country that the whole Sixties movement could have only dreamt about.

I knew absolutely no one in the city and set about trying to meet some people. I would sit in a café in Mala Stranska, reading an English book to indicate my nationality. I'd leave my watch at the hotel and have a pack of cigarettes with no lighter so that I had a couple of introduction methods if I spotted someone that I liked the look of. But there were hardly any foreigners around. For a couple of days I spent some very pleasant hours people-watching as the city paraded herself in front of me and trams and old Skodas rattled past. It was what I had imagined Paris was going to be. There, I had been about fifty years too late. Not here. I got that special feeling that I had arrived at the right time in the right city. For once I was right here, right now. This was the intermediate Prague. Post communism but pre the coachloads of German tourists and planeloads of drunken stag parties. I was determined to soak up as much of it as possible before it all ended.

On my third night I was sitting in my café when two very un-Czech-looking men walked in. By un-Czech I mean that they were not wearing grey anoraks and sporting the hairstyle of a third-year natural sciences student. I got very excited as these were almost the first foreigners that I'd seen up close since I'd arrived. There was little need for props. They were as excited as I was to see a fellow foreigner. They were students, Brian and Steve, from Columbia University in New York. They had been in Prague for a couple of weeks and were already behaving like old hands. We got on well and they invited me to join them that evening. I felt a wave of relief wash over me. I had survived touchdown. I was on my way.

They were off to eat and then to a concert, but not any old concert. They had tickets to see one half of The Velvet Underground play a gig in Bunker, the Politburo's old nuclear bunker that had been turned into a nightclub in a typically Czech touch. I could barely believe it. We grabbed some Czech pizza and made our way to the venue. I managed to buy a ticket outside off a tout for the princely sum of fifty pence. Inside, beer was ten pence a pint and everyone was absolutely smashed. About half an hour after we arrived the two rather less glamorous members of The Velvet Underground, Stirling Morrison and Mo Tucker, took to the stage and delivered a quite spectacular gig. Towards the end, Mo Tucker, the diminutive female drummer, gave a little speech about how the Prague Spring of '68 had been so important to so many people and how thrilled they were that freedom had finally come to the country. People were in tears as she introduced 'Pale Blue Eyes' and dedicated it to 'an extraordinary man who has just become your extraordinary President and who is here tonight, ladies and gentlemen: Václav Havel.' The place erupted as a smallish man in the standard Czech anorak and bad hair stood up about two yards away from me and gave everyone a shy wave. What a country! You could attend a tiny gig by The Velvet Underground and share the mosh pit with the country's President with zero security. I began to think that I might never return to England.

I woke up the next day with a stonking hangover but it didn't seem to matter. My head was still full of images of the night before and I couldn't suppress a little laugh to myself as I had breakfast. I had found somewhere to live in Hradcany, up by the castle. It was the top floor of a private house in the diplomatic quarter, only about ten minutes' walk from the Delegation where I was to start work in a couple of days. The house was owned by a Mrs Klima who spoke no English but managed to communicate through drawing stuff on a blackboard in her kitchen. I guessed, correctly, that she was a teacher. I managed to work out that she wanted the equivalent of twenty pounds a month rent. This seemed more than reasonable. She lived on her own on the ground floor, her son lived in the basement and I had the top floor. We shared a front door but it was very private and I had a pretty good set-up and a great view down to the castle so I was very happy. The decor was simple but liveable with. The only slight irritation was that the entire wall of the sitting room was covered by one enormous photo of Paris and this brought back fresh memories that I didn't really need here in my new life. So, much to Mrs Klima's dismay, I hung a drape over it. Every day she would come upstairs and take the drape down and I would replace it every night. The routine became quite comforting in a weird sort of way.

Come Monday morning I showed up for work at the Delegation. I have to admit to being almost totally ignorant of what the Commission or the Delegation did. Luckily it appeared that most of the staff there were in the same position. The basic idea was that the European Commission, the civil service and powerhouse of the EU, had delegations (basically mini-embassies) in various cities around the world. There was obviously one in each EU capital and there were a couple in places like Washington and Tokyo. But there were also Delegations in most of the former Eastern bloc countries and they were there mainly to coordinate EU reconstruction programmes and aid. This I know now but at the time I had absolutely no clue what I was supposed to be doing and neither did anyone else. My arrival had clearly ruffled a few feathers. It was clear that I had been parachuted in by some important connection so people were careful around me but I didn't really seem to have a defined role. This suited me fine. I took an office at the top of the building and used the facilities to organise my social life. I soon made a small group of friends, mostly ex-pat Brits and Americans, and we would hang out at Jo's Bar which was run by two Americans and was the main meeting point for everyone before a night out. I had a couple of Czech friends who were great but the problem really was the language. I had made enough progress to be able to direct a Czech cabbie fluently towards my home. It was important to make a cabbie think that you might be

Czech as there was a curious fare situation whereby Czechs got charged on rate one, local foreigners on rate two and tourists on the extortionate three. It was an indication of how well your Czech accent was going as to what number the cabbie flicked up on the meter as you got in. I had got the initial directions and hailing chatter so good that I actually got a couple of ones. Unfortunately the moment a conversation started he would lose his temper and flick it onto three. It was all good fun. I took a couple of lessons but didn't have the patience. The very hint of a classroom or homework made me come out in a cold sweat. I determined to muddle through. I'd pick it up in the end. The Czechs that I did know were wonderfully gentle, funny people. There was Hanna, a girl who worked at the Delegation, spoke English better than me and was one of the most poised people that I'd ever met. She was married to a man who specialised in eating disorders, a condition that had tripled in the short time that Czech women had been exposed to Western TV. She had two lovely daughters and they would sometimes invite me back to their place for a meal or we would go out for a drink. I don't think that she really approved of me but I was a curiosity and made her laugh in an otherwise fairly anodyne office populated by worthy Germans and French living a tax-free life of luxury. My boss, Gunther, was a humourless German who looked a little like John Cleese. He definitely didn't approve of me, could clearly spot a slacker when he saw one but he was powerless and so ignored me like a rash that he hoped would eventually go away.

Prague was a fantastically placed city to use as a base to visit Central Europe. On weekends, I'd make trips to Budapest, Munich, Bratislava, Vienna, Krakow and Dresden.

They were all beautiful in their own way but the real plea-sure was that Prague, my home city, was the jewel in the crown. However much I enjoyed visiting other places, I was always thrilled to get back to Bohemia.

One day I got into work and started making my daily social calls as there was a gig on that night and I was trying to organise a good group to go along. Suddenly, there was a knock on my door. It was Gunther.

'*Guten Tag*, Dominic. Are you busy?' he asked with a raised eyebrow, surveying the copy of *Big-Breasted Czech Babes* open on the desk and me, feet up, smoking a fag, my elbow cradling the phone.

'No, no,' I said brazenly. 'Please come in, Gunther. Can I get you a coffee?'

'*Nein danke*, I am here because I need you to represent me this afternoon.' It was clear that this was a last resort as he visibly grimaced as the words left his mouth.

'Sure thing, that would be fine,' I lied, grinning.

'I would not ask you but I have to be in Munich this afternoon and there is no one else here today because of the general council meeting in Strasbourg.' He looked a very worried man.

'Don't worry, Gunther, how hard can it be?' I smiled.

'*Ja, ja*, this is no laughing minute, there is a G8 meeting at the French embassy that you need to attend as Commission representative. You must say nothing, anything that is asked just refer back to Brussels and tell me about it, understood?' He had aged visibly in the last two minutes. 'Also I need you to present the PHARE proposal to the Minister of Culture before that meeting. You know about PHARE, yes?' He looked at me pleadingly.

'Of course I do, Gunther,' I replied, completely ignorant of what he was on about.

'It is simply a formality, you must just hand over the document and tell the Minister that we await his decision. You must not answer any question, simply refer back to Brussels, understood?'

I nodded and smiled. This could actually be fun. I was getting a bit bored sitting in the office and this was a chance to be important. 'Do I get an official car?' I asked.

Gunther looked pained. '*Ja, ja,* you can take Jirji as I will be away. I will let him know.' Gunther looked like a man who knew that he was making an enormous mistake. 'Tell me again what you did before you came here to us?' he asked.

'I dabbled in political journalism in Westminster and on the *International Herald Tribune* before being taken on by MI6 to come here and steal state secrets,' I deadpanned.

'*Ja,* you are joking, yes, very good, but this is no joke, please I beg you, refer everything to Brussels.' He got up to leave the room, a broken man.

'Don't worry, Gunther, I'll refer anything to Mussells,' I laughed.

'*Brussels,*' pleaded Gunther.

'I'm joking, Gunther,' I laughed.

He left the room, pale and muttering to himself. This was going to be fun.

At one o'clock that afternoon, Gunther's huge, tinted 7-Series BMW pulled up outside the front door of the Delegation and his cheery Czech driver Jirji opened the door for me.

'Morning, Mr Dominic, you are business today, yes?' He

beamed. I think he was looking forward to having someone apart from Gunther in the car for a day.

'Hey, Jirji, Ministry of Culture and step on it,' I laughed.

The car shot away from the Delegation and we roared through the mostly empty streets of medieval Prague. We were by far the largest car in the city and the little alleys had not exactly been designed for this monster. Jirji skilfully piloted it through the more tricky areas as I leaned back in the black leather seats and made sure I savoured the moment. I turned the stereo on using the controls in the back seat. Typically it was tuned into 'Gunther FM' and it was playing Dire Straits' 'Romeo and Juliet'. Normally anything by Dire Straits made me physically sick but even they sounded good at this moment. I turned the volume up and we roared on towards the Ministry. Jirji pulled up outside the imposing ministry building at five to two. I straightened my tie and waited for him to open the door. I got out trying to look as insouciant as possible but the truth was that I had suddenly got a little nervous about the whole afternoon since I really did know absolutely nothing about what I was supposed to be doing. Gunther had given me a fat stack of files to read when I first arrived but they had immediately disappeared into the bottom of my office cupboard. I sort of wished now that I'd given them a glance. Undaunted, I strode into the building and, along with a young woman, got into the strange open lift that would take me to the sixth floor. The lift was completely open to the front with no door or railing. It was also open to the wall at the back so simply consisted of a small wooden panel on either side. It was a most peculiar feeling as we were lifted into the eaves of the building and I started to get quite acute vertigo. I tried to look calm but the official was staring at me in a weird way as I felt myself go red and could feel the sweat pouring down the back of my shirt. It was suddenly unbearably hot, I couldn't breathe, and my heart was pounding as though it might burst. I had to get out and, before I knew it, I had stepped out of the front of the peculiar lift into mid air. At this point, if it hadn't been for my belt and the strength of the Nicole Farhi belt hooks, you, dear reader, would have reached the end of this book save a short epitaph by someone I probably didn't like about how he was at a loss as to why anyone had published this book since I had achieved so very little in my life.

As it is, he or she can fuck off. I was caught by one belt hook and hung suspended five floors above the main atrium of the Czechoslovak Ministry of Culture in the middle of a full-blown panic attack. It was not going to be a great afternoon. The woman official, with the help of two beefy security guards, managed to lift me back into the lift and then onto the safety of the sixth floor. My panic had slightly subsided but I was still a little detached. I had been through something similar quite a few times but never at such a crucial moment. It was a bit like an out of body experience where I could hear myself having a normal conversation but was almost an observer, as though I was floating around the event watching it take place.

(Oaksey says that it's just the brain switching off when it can't cope any more. It shuts everything down and goes into autopilot until the situation is calmer. This kind of makes sense but doesn't help when it happens. Oaksey is very good at the diagnosis stuff but doesn't ever really tell you what to do about it. He thinks it's all character building, no gain without pain etc. It can get quite irritating.)

None of this was helping me relax into the role of repre-sentative to the European Commission. Still, nothing ventured, nothing gained. I tried to remember what they had told us at school about running India: be assertive, take control of the situation, you are born to rule. I knew it would all come in useful one day. I was shown into the Minister's room through a small ante-room where three secre-taries sat typing away on ancient typewriters while four or five people sat in a row of chairs against the far wall as though there for a wake. The Minister's office was straight out of a Bond film. It was an enormous room, about eight-hundred square feet, taking up an entire corner of the Ministry building and overlooking the whole of old Prague. The room had a very ornate ceiling and cornicing with three large old chandeliers but, save for a large wooden desk and chair at the end where the Minister sat, the rest of the room was bare. His desk was piled high with papers and envelopes and there was a solitary chair in front of it that I grabbed hold of and sat on before he could even acknowledge my pres-ence. The noise of the chair made him look up from his work and an expression of surprise registered on his face as he looked me up and down. Sodden with sweat, red in the face and barely able to keep eye contact, I must have looked quite a state. This was not good.

He was surprisingly young for a minister, no more than ten years older than me, and he had kind eyes. He looked unlike any other politician that I'd ever seen.

'Hello, Mr Joly, I was expecting Gunther today but I am informed that he has urgent business in Munich? I am honoured to meet his deputy. Have you been in Prague long? We have not met before, I think.'

I struggled to focus and sound normal. 'I have only been here for a month but I love it here,' I stammered, keeping it short and sweet.

'What were you doing before your posting here, were you in Brussels?'

'Yes, yes I was,' I lied for no reason.

'Which DG, 7 or 8? I only ask because I was there two weeks ago and was astonished by the work they do there. I presume that you were on the Czechoslovak desk, you must have known Eric Poitier. Such a brilliant man.'

'Utterly brilliant,' I repeated, lying for no reason. I was now getting in deep and it was my own fault.

'You worked with him for how long?' The Minister seemed unusually interested, was this a trap?

'About three years,' I lied.

'Three years, so you must have been with him through the whole initial stage as well as the current set-up?' he said excitedly.

'Oh yes, right from the initial stuff.' I whimpered, praying that we might get off the subject.

'Then you might just be the man to help me, off the record of course.'

'Of course.' I replied, blankly praying for some earthquake to destroy the building. Was Prague in an earthquake zone? No, I didn't think so. Now if we were in Athens there might be a chance but not here, not in bloody Prague – nothing had disturbed this place for over a thousand years apart from the odd bump of a Catholic landing on the stones far below the castle . . .

'You know Poitier is crucial in determining the Commission's stance on a Czech–Slovak split.' The Minister was staring right at me. 'What is your . . . off the record of course . . . feeling on where he stands on this issue? It would be of great use to us if I could give the President a . . . how you say . . . a steer on this.'

'The President, who, Havel?' I mumbled.

'Yes, he would very much like to know how the Commission views this subject,' said the Minister.

'I met him,' I mumbled. I was losing it.

'Who, Havel?' said the Minister, looking a little surprised.

'Yes, we were at an event together the other evening, we had a good chat about stuff, great man, he's a great man.' I was watching myself blatantly lying to the Minister and I started to chuckle. God, I was totally losing it; I needed some of those Kalms things but it was just me and him. Maybe a coffee? No, that would totally send me over the edge.

'I didn't realise that you knew him,' said the Minister.

'Oh yes, we get on well,' I continued.

'I'm glad to hear it, he is a great man. Did you discuss the separation at all?'

'His wife?' I replied, trying to look concerned.

'The separation of the Czech and Slovak states,' prompted the Minister.

'Oh no,' I said, warming to my new-found clout, 'we never talk work, only music and pottery.'

'Poetry?' asked the Minister, looking puzzled.

'Sorry, yes, I mean poetry, sometimes we talk about pottery but not often, but no we don't talk shop.'

'What would you think that Poitier's and the general Brussels feeling would be about separation?' he tried again.

'Oh, they're . . . we're all for it. Fucking Slovaks, waste of time, dead weights, fuck 'em, you'll be much better off

without them, I'd go for it as soon as possible if I were you
. . . off the record of course.' I put on my best serious look
and it came off well. The Minister looked at me in silence
for a moment before speaking.

'So if I understand you correctly – and to be honest it would
be difficult not to as you speak in the most refreshingly honest
terms – Brussels is in favour of the separation of the Czech
and Slovak states?' The Minister looked at me intently.

'Absolutely, full steam ahead, *vive la différence*, chocks
away.' I'd nearly lost my mind but I was quite enjoying my
assertiveness in a delirious sort of way. The Minister stood
up to indicate that the meeting was over. He shook my
hand warmly and showed me to the door.

'I think that you are a man that we can do business with,'
he said, opening the door.

'I'm certainly not Gorbachev,' I replied, longing to leave.

'So refreshing to meet a straight shooter, *dobry den*,' he
said, using the personalised Czech greeting to say goodbye.

As I was leaving the room, I realised that I still had the folder
Gunther had given me. I pressed it into the Minister's hands
saying, 'Here's the PHARE stuff. You'll love it. It's a great
read.' He took the folder and bolted out of the anteroom.

I got back into the lift with the same female official. She
carefully stood so that she blocked the open front side of the
lift and seemed very tense on the descent to the lobby. She
showed me to the door where Jirji was waiting with the BMW.
I hadn't noticed before that the European flag was flying from
the bonnet. I slumped into the back and Jirji sped off.

'How it go?' he asked, leaning back smiling.

'OK, I think.'

'You want beer?' He indicated a small fridge in the corner

of the car. I leaned in and grabbed a cold bottle of beer. It tasted good.

'Do you want one?' I asked Jirji half-heartedly.

'It's OK, I good,' he replied, showing me a nearly empty bottle twice the size of mine that he was cradling in his lap.

The next meeting was at the French embassy in a second-floor meeting room. There was a representative from each embassy of the G8 countries and they were supposedly reporting to me as the representative of the European Commission to establish how much they were going to donate to certain aid and reconstruction programmes and what they wanted done with various ring-fenced sums. It was all total gibberish to me and I sat there, a little drunk from the strong beer and adrenaline, nodding a lot and staring at the rather good-looking representative from the German embassy. She kept bending over to write and I could get a good glimpse of a pristine white, lacy bra under her heavily starched blouse. Such a shame that she was a Kraut, I thought to myself as a man from Canada waffled on about some university lecturer exchange scheme that they were keen to finance. I nodded away and doodled on my notepad, folding it up towards me and away from the rest of them as though hiding some work from a potential cheat in an exam. The American woman next to me looked a little peeved but I was beyond caring. I was bored and wanted nothing better than to go and have a drink by the river with the German woman. I wondered idly whether she was married.

'Mr Joly, would you sum up please . . .' The Italian man was looking at me; everyone in the room was looking at me. 'We need Brussels' go-ahead for the most urgent projects and a long-term view on the others,' the Italian continued.

I stood up and then realised that no one else had stood up to speak but it was an instinctive thing from the debating society at school. Not that I had been much good at that. There was the disastrous attempt at a balloon debate where you had to persuade people not to throw you out of a balloon. I was Robinson Crusoe and the whole school voted unanimously to chuck me out after my first lame speech . . . Everyone was still staring at me.

'The answer, gentlemen, is no. No to each and every proposal that you have brought to me here today. Obviously I shall refer everything back to Brussels but I can tell you here and now that nothing will be granted. I am very disappointed in the level of commitment offered here today.' I sat down and pretended to write something down. The Italian man looked as though he'd been punched in the face. The Canadian was dumbstruck and I thought that I could detect a hint of a smile on the German woman's face, maybe there was a chance . . . She stood up.

'Ladies and gentlemen, since my colleague and husband Gunther is not here today, he has sent along his colleague and intern Mr Joly to report back to him. Perhaps there has been some sort of misunderstanding here but I suggest that we all await Gunther's return next week before we proceed any further.' She looked at me with cold, hard, Teutonic eyes. 'That should be all for today, do we agree?' She sat down and started to arrange her papers as everyone else got up to leave. I got up and walked out, looking straight ahead. I got into the car and told Jirji to drive me to the Café Mozart under the Charles Bridge. He joined me for a couple of beers and soon the whole afternoon became a distant memory. It had been a fairly mixed first excursion into the world of international diplomacy.

No one said much to me at the Delegation from then on. Gunther never spoke to me again, which was quite good really as I didn't have any work to do and I started to come in later and later only to leave earlier and earlier. I rang Philby in London but he didn't have much to say. I had a feeling that our relationship was coming to an end since I had finally got into a position of some use to him and had completely blown it. He hinted that my salary might be coming to a halt very soon as there were 'budgetary re-assessments going on'. I asked him what the deal with the Delegation gig was.

'You're secure there for nine months or so but then I can't really guarantee anything.'

'That's fine,' I told him. 'Can I hang on to my degree?'

'Of course you can,' he replied and then said that he would have to go. He told me to contact him when I was back in London as 'you never know' but not to rely on anything concrete. We said our goodbyes. I was fond of Philby, he'd helped me out a lot and it was a shame that I hadn't ever produced anything for him. But still, as he often said, that's the espionage game. I wasn't really sure what he was talking about but it made me feel better.

I found a great little place called Café Savoy. It was just on the castle side of the river but a bit further downstream than Mala Strana. It had high, painted ceilings and enormous windows allowing me to people-watch in warm seclusion. They served big frothy creamy coffees, good beer and a weird mixture of Czech delicacies like zmazny cir (fried cheese) and a strange curried chicken and rice thing that wasn't really curry and I couldn't swear to be chicken but tasted good. It was here, two weeks later, that I noticed the front-page headline of the *Prague Post*: 'Czech/Slovak Split to Go Ahead, Provisional Date of New Year's Day Announced'. I wondered whether I'd had any influence in the matter. I chuckled to myself and ordered a celebratory beer. It wasn't every day that you had a hand in splitting a country up. The waitress brought me a large Czech beer and a freezing pint glass. They really knew how to serve the stuff here. I gave the waitress, a thin, dark-haired girl, a smile. She smiled back. She was new and I hadn't seen her working here before. I thanked her in broken Czech: '*Dykwyu.*' There were so many variations of the ending it was all bollocks but she got my drift. She smiled at me and said, 'You welkime' in a heavy Czech accent. Her English was as crap as my Czech. I liked her immediately. To make conversation I asked her where she had learned her English. She looked at me blankly. We had clearly already travelled to the frontiers of her linguistic abilities. She was really pretty but dressed like a Victorian housemaid as Czech waitresses tended to be. I smiled at her and she smiled back before returning to the kitchen. I started going to the Savoy almost every day after that and felt really sad when she wasn't working. On the fifth day I asked her her name and, after some clarificatory hand gestures, worked out that it was Ludmilla. Not the most attractive of names but I'd heard worse. I did a lot of smiling at her and, a couple of weeks later, I brought in a Czech/English phrase book. Leafing through it, I got the impression that it must have been published quite some time ago. I decided to just jump in.

'Do you know of a blacksmith where I can get my horses shod and the axle of my carriage mended?' She looked puzzled and then laughed. I ploughed on: 'My travelling companion is injured and I have left him high up in the pass. Could you alert the nearest mountain rescue unit?' Again she laughed. Her eyes lit up and her nose wrinkled, sending little laughter lines down the sides of her cheeks. I sensed victory. Then I played my trump card: 'Would you be interested in joining me for afternoon tea; my aunt will happily chaperone the encounter?' She laughed and then stared at me, biting her lip, unsure as to whether I was serious or not. I looked at her seriously and nodded encouragingly. She blushed and nodded in shy acceptance. She showed me her watch and pointed to seven o'clock and then to the back door of the café. I grinned and left her with: 'The Danube is rising fast; should we seek higher ground?' I skipped out of the café. My first date since Mandy. I was very excited.

I returned to the Savoy at twenty-five to seven and hung around the back door until she finally appeared at about five past. We smiled at each other and started to walk down the riverbank towards Mala Strana. I stopped using the phrase book as it really didn't have anything of use in it unless we were going to go on a Victorian mule expedition for a date. We tried to act stuff out but it wasn't clear whether we were actually getting across what we needed to.

I think she was twenty-five and had a university degree in either medicine or gardening. She lived with her parents in a flat in Vinhorady, a nice area on the other side of town. She liked Phil Collins and she either loved or hated Supertramp, I couldn't work it out, every time I tried to sing a song of theirs her face would contort into an odd shape. I think she liked them but am still not sure. We had supper at a strange little place called the Knights of Malta. It was an old Czech restaurant deep in the bowels of an ancient building near Mala Stranska. We had trout, a strange local delicacy for such a landlocked country but there were plenty of lakes and rivers about, and it was delicious. We drank some pretty revolting local white wine but it did the trick, for me certainly. We were soon sitting under one of the statues on the Charles Bridge watching the world go by. We huddled close together because of the cold and it felt good. There didn't seem any rush to do anything. It was as though there was some sort of understanding between us. We went to Jo's Bar for a drink and played chess for an hour or so, not saying anything but doing a lot of smiling. Eventually the bar closed and I walked her home, all the way to Vinhorady. I kissed her on her doorstep and she went inside. I walked home in the moonlight through the empty medieval streets with a gentle cushion of virgin snow making an echoey squeaking sound beneath my feet. We had hardly said an intelligible word to each other all night but I was sure that this was something pretty special. Also I hadn't met anyone else in Prague, which might have influenced things.

We met up pretty much every night for the next month. My Czech didn't get any better and her English was non-existent but we got on. We laughed a lot and she would occasionally stay over at my place. One night we got back and I turned on my telly, I wanted to show her *Spinal Tap* and see what she made of it. I figured it was quite visual so she might enjoy it. Unfortunately my TV was somehow hooked into the same aerial as Mrs Klima's weird son's telly. He lived in the basement and hardly ever came out. I had seen him once in the garden shooting at the traffic on the road far below with an air rifle. I hadn't said anything at the time, as there didn't seem to be anything I could do about it. I knew that he was trouble.

That evening he'd clearly decided to watch some really quite extraordinarily hardcore bestial pornography that gave me a little shock when I turned on my television. Ludmilla got an even bigger shock when she saw a woman go down on a very well-endowed horse whilst a man in the background with a dodgy moustache pleasured a goat with a dodgy beard. She looked at me in absolute horror and I struggled hard to explain in hand signals that this was not my idea of a night out and that some mutant in the basement was responsible for it. I don't think that she understood. I never attempted to watch TV again when anyone else was in the room.

The next morning as we left to go to work we bumped into mutant basement boy in the driveway. He was dragging a large plastic bag down towards the skip in the street. To me it was a clear case of chop and kill. He had obviously lured someone into his gimp room, drugged them, raped them whilst wearing a horse's head and then killed them in a pique of guilt, and was now disposing of the evidence by chopping them up and putting them in the skip and we'd stumbled upon him in mid-act. We were dead for sure. I was certain that if the body was found it would be me that would get the blame, the solitary foreigner who never brought friends back, kept himself to himself. The only person who'd ever been in my flat socially had seen bestiality on my telly. She'd turn on me like they all did when push came to shove. I was fucked, I was going to be fitted up for a bestiality sex killing in the middle of bloody Bohemia and there was nothing that I could do . . .

'He control flyplane,' said Ludmilla.

'What?' I replied, my mind still racing with pictures of the gimp pit. I hadn't noticed that she was talking to the Prague Ripper.

She mimed an airplane and him sitting at a computer screen; he started making bleeping noises and then simulated a crashing sound, then they both burst out laughing. I didn't know what the fuck they were on about and started walking off but Ludmilla was still talking to him and I had to wait by the gate and then give him a wave through clenched teeth as we walked off. He continued dragging the bag of body parts down towards the skip. I gave him a quick glance and then looked at the bag and back at him to let him know that I knew his game. He waved again and shouted something at Ludmilla.

'What did he say?' I asked her, making a questioning sign with my hands like a gurning idiot. She made another plane crashing sound and I gave up. I had started to have enough of being abroad, I wanted to go back home, somewhere where I could fucking communicate with people. I turned to Ludmilla.

'Do you want to come and live with me in London?'

She looked at me blankly. I made a plane sound and indicated travel by running down the road and then doing a Lambeth Walk type thing to indicate Britain. It was useless. She just started making the plane crash sounds again and started laughing. When I got to the office I got out the useless phrase book and rang the Café Savoy.

'Ludmilla,' I kept repeating until she finally came to the phone.

'Ahoy,' she said, using a Czech greeting that made everyone sound like a gay sailor.

'Ahoy,' I replied and then launched into some phrase-book Czech: 'I intend to make a long journey back to my homeland. I need the correct supplies for you to come.' I tried to splice two phrases together and was pretty sure that it hadn't worked. I tried again: 'I must return from whence I came. Your people have shown me great generosity. Maybe one day our peoples will not be at war together.' I heard her gasp and realised that this sounded wrong as well. I ran and got Jana from the next office and got her to translate: 'Tell her that I think I'm in love with her and that I want her to come back to London with me.' Jana relayed the information down the phone. There was a pause.

'She wants to know how much money you make a year?' said Jana, holding her hand over the mouthpiece in a frankly pointless way since Ludmilla couldn't understand a word she was saying. I hesitated for a moment. Jana told me that this was a fairly normal question in Prague. I told Jana to tell her that it was about £100,000 a year. If I was going to lie then I might as well make sure that I'd seal the deal. Jana told Ludmilla the information with a slight frown on her face. There was another pause and then Jana turned to me.

'She's packing her bags.'

Things Fall Apart

LUDMILLA WAS BLOWN away by London. I tried to explain that Hounslow wasn't really the high point of the city but, as she didn't understand a word that I was saying, I let her gibber out of the taxi window whilst I tried to work out where we could live. My useful income from MI6 had now been stopped and we were pretty much penniless. I had arranged to stay with a friend near Portobello Road but I had to sort something else out fast. The house was a tall pink building parallel to the market and our room was a damp cupboard-like thing in the basement with a great view of a dead yucca plant and a rusty barbecue that cluttered up the six square feet of concrete that W11 inhabitants call gardens.

We went for a walk down Portobello, starting at the posh end with the very expensive antique shops frequented by fat Americans in white polo necks with 'mug me' signs hanging round their necks. The walk was one of my favourites because it deteriorated so dramatically as it went on. Posh antiques gave way to a fairly grubby fruit and veg market followed by a standard bric-a-brac type area where you could buy rubbish Indian garb and a poster of Bob Marley for a fiver. My favourite part was right at the end, in the walled-off section leading up to Golborne Road where the stuff started to get a bit desperate and you could buy a single shoe if you so desired.

Ludmilla was transfixed; I pointed out Nick Cave leaning against a wall talking to an enormous Rastafarian but she looked completely blank. Under the Westway we saw a grubby-looking Mick Jones from The Clash riffling through some second-hand books at a stall. Again, she seemed nonplussed. She finally screeched with delight when a bedraggled-looking Jason Donovan walked by, pushing a small child in a pram. I was fascinated that she might have known who Jason Donovan was. Surely *Neighbours* hadn't reached Prague? I sang the theme tune to her and she gave me a huge smile and started singing it in Czech. It was our first major cultural breakthrough and very exciting. We actually got on pretty well in our fragmented communication. We never argued, as we could never discuss anything with enough depth or passion to disagree about it. At least I now knew she loved *Neighbours*.

I needed a job, and quick. After a couple of calls to some old school friends I found a vacancy in a big private equity firm in the City. I had absolutely no idea what this entailed but the friend I'd rung had been the thickest boy at school and he'd just been made a director, so how hard could it be? I had a perfunctory interview in which a large, thick-necked man asked me, in some detail, about the hooker situation in Prague. He looked like he should have been playing second-row for an international rugby team (it subsequently turned out that he did). My second interviewer did three rather unsubtle lines of cocaine during the interview, attempting to hide the fact by putting his hand in front of the stuff as he made enormous snorting noises and strafed the desk with his nose. They asked me about my school and my connection there. After about fifteen minutes they offered me a job with a starting salary of twenty-five thousand pounds a year. I nodded in agreement, still unsure what the job was, and skipped back to our dungeon to tell Ludmilla. Of course, she didn't understand so I drew some dollar signs on a piece of paper and gave her the thumbs up. She smiled back but since she was under the assumption that I earned £100,000 a year she could have assumed that I'd just mugged a granny for all she knew. I wondered what it was that she thought that I did.

I rented a large two-bedroom flat on All Saints Road. It was a lot cheaper than anywhere else but I only discovered when we moved in that this was because it was on the 'front line'. Basically this was West London's pharmacy cum knocking shop. Whatever you wanted, whether it was hookers or heroin, you made a beeline to my road. This obviously didn't make for a particularly strong Neighbourhood Watch scheme. At night Ludmilla and I would try to get to sleep to the sound of hookers slapping and punching each other whilst vicious-looking dealers kicked two shades of shit out of drunken Sloanes who'd unwisely wandered down the road trying to buy some marijuana. On our fifth night in our new home, there was an unusually loud argument, even by this street's standards. I looked out of the window to see a man brandishing a large pistol put nine bullets into another man sitting in an old, white Mercedes. I stood transfixed as the shooter calmly put the pistol back into his pocket and wandered off down the road. On the opposite side of the street every window was lit up and faces peered out hesitantly, anxiously trying to ascertain just how much lower the street had sunk. I rang the police and reported the incident and they were there in minutes. The whole area was sealed off as the victim, who was still alive, was gingerly taken out and put into an ambulance. I drifted off to sleep and dreamt of Arthur for the first time in ages. He was angry – maybe it was the gunfire.

'What are you doing? Living with a foreigner, dull, regular job – you are destined for greatness, great things, you're throwing it all away. Burn, you must burn like the sun!' He was holding up my old cat by its neck and started bashing the thing against a brick wall. 'This is what's going to happen to you if you don't get your act together. Arise, move on, do something, or I'll fucking . . .' I woke up and turned on the television to try to re-focus, only to see a live report from right underneath my window. The reporter was going on about how 'As the violence spirals out of control, police are now openly saying that this area of West London is almost a no-go area for them.' Fucking great, I'd really made a good decision to move in here. I cheered myself up by pouring a saucepan of freezing cold water over the reporter's head from the window just as he was finishing his report. I finally managed to have a very exciting dream about Ludmilla and her two imaginary identical sisters. Unfortunately I was in some bizarre latex costume being beaten with eucalyptus leaves by a large, hairy man. I tried to channel that one away but it was a strange night.

The next morning two plain-clothes officers came round and took a statement from me. I was quite proud of my ability to recall exactly what happened and, not wanting to look stupid, made up bits I wasn't sure of. When they got to the bit where the gunman walked off I told them that I had only been able to see him for a couple of yards but that all the people on the other side of the road would have had a much better view than me.

'What other people, sir?' said one of the police officers, looking up at me.

'Every window had a face in it, there must be dozens of witnesses,' I replied.

'I'm afraid not, sir. You are currently the only witness to this incident – we'll obviously be needing you in court when this comes to trial.' His mouth cracked into a reassuring smile.

It was bloody omertà. I hadn't realised that there were various unwritten rules on this street and I'd most likely just broken the most important one. I'd become a bloody supergrass. I'd be strung up from the nearest lamp-post if anyone found out. I got rid of the police as quickly as possible and decided to try and ignore any further contact that they made with me.

The following Monday I started work in the City. I say work as I don't really know what else to call it but I did absolutely nothing at all. The job, as far as I could make out, was to make wads of cash for people by somehow buying and holding things called shares on the stock market. That is genuinely all I know. No one really told me what to do and I simply hung around a large desk full of City types and spent a lot of time on the phone to friends. It soon became apparent that women were not really welcome in this environment. Men hung around in packs and went for three-hour boozy lunches where they leered at women and spoke of their previous night's conquests. Everyone took kilos of cocaine and the cubicles were constantly full of three or four men snorting away before returning to their desks to wallow in the 'sea of me'. On the third day I was invited into a cubicle by members of my desk. It was clearly a test to see if I would fit in. I took three fat lines and spent the next two hours gibbering on about how I was born to be something special and how much I loved my new job, whatever it was. Arthur would have been proud of me. I was in a completely alien environment full of cocky, misogynist, drug-taking idiots: I fucking loved it.

The pattern continued for a couple of months. I would turn up at work, hang around for a couple of hours until someone cracked open the drugs and then we'd all go off for increasingly long liquid lunches. No one seemed to care how long we took, what we did or when we did it. I could only assume that there was some other department in the company that did all the real work as none seemed to be done in mine. Maybe the whole company was simply a front for some Colombian drug cartel trying to launder their money. Whatever it was I didn't care. The facts were that I had a job that paid well and I didn't have to do anything apart from copious amounts of drink and drugs. Ludmilla didn't seem to notice that I was coming back from work wired and drunk, but since we didn't really 'do' communication, it wasn't that surprising. She had got a job in a café overlooking Portobello Road. The owner was Czech and spoke as little English as she did. The place was quite well known for having a great view of the market but zero chance of getting what you ordered. It had become a tradition that, on a hot day, you turned up, sat in the sun, tried to order something, put up with whatever destiny brought to your table and laughed at the tourists getting in a tizz. They always gave up in the end. Ludmilla seemed very happy there, though most of the time I was too off my tits to notice.

Work, or what passed for it, continued apace. I had started to buy my own drugs off the dealer who worked on reception. You turned up in the morning, picked up an envelope from the front desk, got yourself topped up and then headed out for a liquid breakfast. Lunch had become such a long time to wait for. We used to go to a pub in Smithfield Market that opened early for the market workers. I began to almost forget to go to the office itself as breakfast rolled into lunch and the sun came out and we would lie about in packed City parks watching other office workers strip to their pants and go lobster pink in that peculiarly British way.

I was flung into a real panic one evening at home when I saw two policemen standing at my door. In a paranoid panic I flushed three grams of cocaine down the loo before going to the door trying to look as normal as possible. It turned out that they were not there to bust me but to make sure that I had got the letters telling me that I was due in court the next week as a witness to the shooting. I hadn't read any of the letters but I was so relieved that it wasn't anything more serious that I readily agreed.

The next week, after a quick trip to the Old Bailey loos, I was outside the courtroom being briefed by two policemen about what was to happen. I told them that I hoped that I could be of help but I was nervous about being identified as a 'grass'. They said that my address would not be mentioned so not to worry. My chemical sidekicks were making me very cocky and I strode into court brazenly and took the stand.

The prosecution barrister asked me whether I had good eyesight. When I told him that I had 20/20 vision he asked whether I'd mind taking a test. He showed me a picture of All Saints Road and asked me to read the licence plate on a distant car. I started chuckling. The car he pointed out was the one that Ludmilla and I had just purchased. I started to enjoy everyone looking at me, I felt important. The interrogation went fine until the defence barrister asked me to verify that I lived . . . and he read out my exact address . . . I looked around the court, there was no one there who cared and I relaxed as I realised that it wasn't likely that the local pimps read court proceedings. I verified that I lived there and proceeded to retell my story, further embellishing it with unnecessary details. When it was all over, I felt good. I was thanked by the judge for being a 'brave' witness, which I didn't quite understand, but I smiled and nearly waved before turning to leave the stand and exit the court. It was at that moment that I noticed the mezzanine section of the court containing the public gallery which I hadn't noticed before, having walked underneath it to reach the witness stand. I stood transfixed as I took in the rows and rows of dour-looking Rastafarians and local ne'er-do-wells staring at me from the packed gallery. I raced from the court and straight home where I rang the local locksmith and ordered three more locks for my front door. I never walked down the street alone again. I didn't tell Ludmilla about it as I didn't want to upset her and also because I still couldn't communicate with her about anything deeper than cornflakes.

After a couple of months in the City I was taking a huge amount of drugs on a daily basis. I would do cocaine alongside about fifteen pints in the daytime and then start trying to come down in the evening by smoking so much grass that I was in danger of turning into a bush. I would finish the evening with half a bottle of brandy before falling into bed in a stupor and getting a sort of sleep before starting all over again. Even the people at work started to notice that I had accelerated past them in levels of consumption in a very short time. The City wasn't the sort of place where anyone would worry about that sort of thing. They simply complimented me on the fact that I had become one of the top 'caners' in the company. It made me realise that things were getting a bit out of hand. I didn't do anything about it, though, just carried on down the same road.

I knew I was in trouble when Arthur started appearing on a regular basis. He wouldn't leave me alone. At night I'd be working my way through a bottle of Famous Grouse and he'd be sitting next to me egging me on: 'That's it, boy, glug it down, fuck 'em all, you're special, you're different from the rest of 'em, you've got balls, that's my boy, finish it off.' He'd be sitting on the sofa, slouched like an uncouth cousin, his undercarriage hanging out, puffing on an enormous cigar. He looked happy for once and that was a worrying sign. He was normally ranting at me, getting at me, but he was happy as Larry.

'Not going to bed, are you? What, turned into a poof suddenly, have we? There's plenty more where that came from, crack open another one, after all, it's not like you need sleep and I don't want you rutting with that foreign slapper, it's not healthy.' Arthur spat and a large gob of phlegm hit the framed picture of Ludmilla that sat on top of the mantelpiece. 'Fucking no-good slapper, you know she's cheating on you with anything in trousers, she'll take you down, you watch,' he snarled. I passed out, which was probably a good thing as paranoia was setting in and I kept thinking that I could see nine-foot Rastafarians with machetes out of the window, hissing 'grassssssssss, grasssss,' and making throat-slitting signs across their necks. Ludmilla and her identical sisters were going down on them as their yellowy eyes drilled bullet holes in my temple. I was in real trouble.

Things came to a head very soon. After a particularly heavy day in the City I apparently decided to go and 'sort out' some bar-tender who'd refused me a drink the night before for being too drunk. No one went with me from work and I ended up being badly beaten up by the barman and a couple of his cronies. They left me in the alley behind the bar and I must have crawled out into the main road as I remember a car screeching to a stop and someone pulling me into the back of it. I think it was a cab driver and he took me to the nearest hospital. Once there, I was wheeled into A&E and, after a two-hour wait, was seen by a doctor. After a couple of tests he must have realised what he was dealing with. He told me that I was going to need specialist help and not to worry, they were going to help me. He gave me an injection and told me to relax. I needed some rest. I suddenly felt very calm for the first time in years. I thanked him and smiled before I drifted off into a gorgeous sleep.

When I opened my eyes I blinked hard, trying to focus amidst the bright lights and whiteness surrounding me. A face was peering at me, a face that I knew well but couldn't place.

'Uh, huh, he seems to be back with us, great stuff,' said the face to someone I couldn't see.

'Uh hi, welcome back to the world, feller, looks like you got saved in the nick of time. You were in quite a bad way for a while there,' continued the face. I suddenly realised why I knew the fucker. It was Sir Cliff Richard. Oh Jesus, had I died and gone to hell?

'Where the fuck am I?' I shouted, trying to look over Sir Cliff's shoulder.

'Uh huh, calm down, buddy, you're in a very special

place, you're in The Priory.' Sir Cliff took an involuntary step backwards, wary of the aggression in my voice.

The Priory . . . How the fuck had I got here, the nuthouse for celebs with 'nervous exhaustion'? Who the fuck had sorted this out? Why was I here and what the fuck was Sir Cliff Richard doing in my room?

'What the fuck are you doing in my room and how did I get here?' I sat up as I spoke and spotted another figure in the corner of the room, hairy and also familiar. 'Fucking hell, Dave Lee Travis, what the fuck is going on here, is this some weird cult centre I've been kidnapped to?' My mind was racing, what the fuck had happened to me?

'Calm down and let me explain,' said Sir Cliff. 'Your company has health insurance that pays for you being here so don't worry about the financial side. DLT and I are here as voluntary helpers. We come here twice a week and just chat to people, try to sort stuff out with them.'

'What? And that's supposed to make people feel better, is it?' I blurted out and then felt bad because they looked really hurt.

'Maybe we should leave him for a bit, get the doc in and then he can give us a shout if he wants to talk later, Cliffy?' said DLT.

'Good idea,' said Sir Cliff.

'Give us a shout if you need anything, we're here until five and then we're off to the Wine Bar of the Year do at the Dorchester, should be lots of fun.' Sir Cliff and DLT slipped out of the room and closed the door behind them. The room was nice, really nice. It had a vaguely clinical feel to it but the furniture was classy. There was a telly and a decent bathroom; it was like a good four-star hotel. I leaned back onto the pillows and promptly fell asleep again. When I woke up there was a doctor-looking guy taking my blood pressure and a pretty nurse was sitting in the corner writing something down on a clipboard.

'Hello, how are you feeling?' asked the doctor, taking the wraparound blood pressure thing off my arm.

'Fine, thanks, where's Cliff Richard?' I asked.

'Yes, sorry they were here when you woke up, must have been a bit of a shock. They like to welcome new people and they can be quite insistent. They love it when someone comes in on a Monday or a Wednesday night as they get to do the meet-and-greet thing.' The doctor nodded towards the nurse and gave her some reading that she scrawled down. She then got up and left the room and the doctor turned back to me. 'Right, you are in here to be treated for severe addictive behaviour towards narcotics, particularly cocaine and alcohol. You are in no way forced to stay here but I would recommend a period of treatment of a minimum of one month and possibly a lot longer. Your company's health programme will pick up the tab so you might as well lie back, relax and think about getting yourself back together. Anyone who needs to know about you being here has been contacted and told that you have "nervous exhaustion". It's up to you to tell anyone about why you're actually here. The only slight problem we had was contacting your wife . . . Ludmina, is it?'

'Ludmilla, and she's not my wife, just my girlfriend.'

'Yes, well, we're having a slight communication problem. We've rung three times but no one can seem to get the message across, her English isn't too good, I take it.'

'No, it's non-existent unless you want to order a coffee and even then you'd be best not to specify.'

'Well, why don't you give her a ring and let her know what's going on and she can come and see you?'

'I don't speak a word of Czech, I have no idea how to communicate with her, certainly not how to tell her about this.'

'Don't worry then,' said the doctor, 'I'm sure we can sort something out. The important thing is for you to get better. If you feel up to it there's a chat session at four this afternoon just down the corridor. Just pop in and I'll introduce you to everyone.' He smiled and left the room. I turned on the telly but wasn't really watching; my head was spinning – how the fuck had it all come to this?

At about five to four the pretty nurse popped her head round my door and asked me whether I felt up to a chat session. Since I didn't have a clue what it was, I decided to go along and have a shufti. I hadn't even left my room yet so I wanted to have a look around. She led me down a long corridor into a large room that looked a bit like a gym. At one end were about ten table tennis tables. At the other end was a tiny stage and some curtains. The rest of the room just had rows of seats all facing the stage. The seats were about half full. There must have been about thirty people in total. I immediately spotted Cliff and DLT on the stage. They nodded to me and DLT pointed to an empty seat in the front row. As I sat down Sir Cliff asked everyone to welcome me, a new patient, and to tell me, one by one, why they were there. Of the thirty patients present about fifteen were household names. It would be unfair of me to name them but I can give hints.

The first to stand up was a well-known sports personality, a footballer – no big surprise there. He announced that he was there for an addiction to sex with inanimate objects. I didn't quite understand what that meant but he proceeded to go into quite extraordinary detail about how hard it was for him to pass a fruit and veg stall without getting over excited. He said that he'd always had problems getting girlfriends and had been teased about having an avocado instead of a security blanket as a kid. DLT nodded sympathetically and called on the next person to stand up. There were a couple of housewives addicted to painkillers, then a very famous newsreader who confessed to an addiction to getting dressed up and exposing himself in the background of colleagues' pieces to camera. He'd check to see where reporters were scheduled to be and then turn up and do his business before returning to the studio and reading the news in the evening as though nothing had happened. He said that he loved the excitement of it all, as well as being a good way of screwing up colleagues' reports. His blonde hair glistened with excitement as he told us of his exploits. I was in shock, these were like the biggest showbiz stories I'd ever read about and here they were, these famous people, letting it all hang out in front of a group of unwell strangers. I suppose that the only explanation was that there was just so much weirdness coming out in that room that no one would ever believe it, even the most lurid of tabloids.

The stories continued fast and furious; the MTV presenter who could only present shows by having her mother read the script into an earpiece which she then duly parroted on screen. Apparently she couldn't read and had become addicted to eyedrops in the hope that this might help. An Irish pop star stood up and told the group that he could only achieve climax by having postmen write obscenities in thick black marker on the back of his legs. A radio phone-in star admitted that he kept the number of callers who annoyed him and would then call them up to two hundred times at night and just say 'you're wrong' before hanging up. The non-celebrities had such everyday addictions to drink, drugs, painkillers, it must have made them feel an awful lot better listening to this litany of celebrity despair. Maybe that was half the point.

A French-sounding woman stood up. She had clearly been in some sort of industrial accident as she was hideously scarred and her face was almost melted together. She spoke movingly about how she had got her life back together after a horrific road accident in Paris. People nodded sympathetically. She went on to recount how she had almost recovered when the person responsible for the road accident had stalked her and viciously attacked her in a nightclub causing her third-degree burns. At that moment I realised that it was Claudine and that I'd better get the fuck out of the room before she recognised me. When she sat down Sir Cliff asked me to stand up and tell everyone what I was in for. I cupped my hands over my face and pretended to break down and ran from the room. I'd have to avoid that particular group during my stay.

That evening I managed to get through to Ludmilla and had a very curious conversation. I was worried that she might have got hold of some of my stash as she didn't make much sense. Her English seemed to have come on a bit despite quite a heavy American accent.

Me: Ludi, hello . . . I am in hospital . . . no come home for a while.

Ludi: We've got a strike on the main field. It's a big one, might take days to cap.

Me: Hello . . . Ludi . . . it's me, Domski. What are you talking about? I'm in hospital.

Ludi: Goddamn it if your daddy was still alive he'd whip your hide.

Me: My daddy is still alive and how come you're speaking English and what are you talking about?

Ludi: I'll be out at the ranch for a while. I gotta think about things.

Me: I honestly don't know what the fuck you're on about, have you touched my grass?

Ludi: Bye, honey.

I put the phone down in a state of some confusion. The last time I'd managed to communicate with Ludmilla she'd barely been able to string two words together. Now she was using whole sentences of complete nonsense.

Over the next couple of weeks I was faced with a daily diet of one-on-one sessions and group discussions about why we indulged in drugs and alcohol and what might be the real reason, plus the occasional bewildering telephone conversation with Ludmilla. It was pretty much common sense but it helped having people lay it all out right in front of you and I soon saw that what I was doing was trying to blot out the fact that I hadn't actually achieved anything in life. To be honest, I didn't really see that but they told me that that was my problem and I felt that they must know what they were talking about. It was made clear to me that I must not go back to the City as it was an unhealthy environment for someone with my predilections to hang out in. They wanted me to find a job in an area where I wouldn't be tempted by illicit drugs and alcohol, wouldn't face excessive stress and would be surrounded by kind, supportive people. I chose TV.

The main inspiration was a chat with DLT. He kept pointing out what an amazing place The Priory was for networking. I realised that he had a point. With so many vulnerable, powerful people in here, how could one fail to get one to employ you? I started to befriend my fellow inmates. I did have some experience, with my political TV background, but I fancied doing something lighter and focused on the 'entertainment' inmates. I grew quite close to a couple of TV producers in for cocaine addiction and spent most of the day playing table tennis. Everyone played fucking table tennis. It was unbelievable. I would play about five hours a day. At times the place felt more like some Chinese training camp than a treatment centre.

I got on well with the producers. We had quite a lot in common as they both lived in the Notting Hill area and we hung out in a couple of the same places. They were older than me and had quite a few hits under their respective belts and I felt confident that they might be able to help me out.

My main therapist was a man who would become very important to me: Oaksey Maseltov. He was of Russian extraction, from Odessa. His family, Mencheviks, had fled to Britain in 1918. He was very unlike how I imagined this sort of therapist would be. He had a coarse sense of humour and liked a drink. He was basically quite normal but had a fantastic way of putting you at ease so that you revealed a lot more than you normally might. He got your defences down and really reached the truth. He would encourage me to write down pages of A4 about my life and to read them over and try to analyse what was good and what was bad about events. I found this profoundly dull but he insisted and after a while I started to quite enjoy it.

Oaksey would be my point of contact once I was on the outside and I would report any relapse to him so it was important that we got on. Even better, because he spoke Russian he could communicate with Ludmilla. I was unaware that all Czechs spoke fluent Russian, since it had been compulsory to teach it in school. Most Czechs refused to speak it because it was the language of the occupier and if you asked them what language they spoke they would never mention Russian. He rang Ludmilla and had a long chat with her as I sat in his office terrified as to what he was telling her. When he got off the phone he was smiling. 'That's a good woman you've got there, she's very funny.'

'Is she, that's good, what did you talk to her about?' I asked nervously.

'I filled her in on the situation and she's totally fine about it all, she knows that you are a high earner and face a lot of stress; she says that in Prague it would have been four bottles of vodka a day. She says that she can't wait for you to come home and she's coming in to see you tomorrow. She also wonders if you can pay off some of her credit card bills while you're in here as they're getting quite big apparently.'

'Credit cards?' I squeaked. 'I didn't know that she had any.'

'She said that she had about five on the go, they kept arriving in the post,' said Oaksey.

'I'm not really a high earner, I just told her that,' I confessed.

'Oh dear, well, we'd better start sorting that out as well.' Oaksey gave me a wink. I liked Oaksey.

The following day I had my first proper conversation with Ludmilla. We sat in Oaksey's office and he translated as we asked each other pretty much everything that we'd wanted to know since we met. I left out intimate bits but unfortunately she didn't.

'She's reasonably happy with your performance in bed but ideally would have liked a better-endowed man,' said Oaksey to me, deadpan.

'Can you tell her that some things are best left between us even if we can't communicate that well? Is she happy in England? Are things OK between us?' I asked, gritting my teeth.

'Things are fine. Apparently she has yet to see your main house which she assumes you are doing up at the moment but she is enjoying working and seeing London and she thinks that you are nice to her and don't beat her like her last boyfriend, which she is thankful for.' Oaksey winked at me again and I wasn't sure if he was joking. 'She wants to know when you are coming home and I told her that you can probably be out of here in a week if that's OK with you.' Oaksey looked right at me.

'Yes, that's great news, I'll see her next week. I can't wait.'

'Also it appears that someone has written something in paint in huge letters on the front of your flat.' He turned to Ludmilla and asked her something in Russian. 'It appears that they've written "you gonna die, honky grass". She wants to know what that's all about?'

I managed to look calm and told Oaksey to assure Ludmilla that it was just local kids mucking about, it was that sort of area . . . that's why I loved it . . . a real melting pot . . . such fun . . . Oaksey waffled on for another couple of minutes to Ludmilla in Russian before saying goodbye. It made me feel a bit sensitive but I didn't press the issue and just smiled. I made a mental note to move as soon as possible when I got out. That night I slipped out of The Priory for the first time since I'd been there. The two TV producers, a sports reporter and I ended up in a nearby pub. We got completely hammered and had a blast. I supposed that we all sort of wanted to get rid of our addictions but there was a limit. A man still needed a drink now and then and it felt really good. One of the producers asked me what I was going to do when I got out. I decided to chance my arm and said that I was going to give TV a go and did they have any suggestions? I tried to look casual about it but I knew that this was my moment. He laughed and told me that he was about to do some comedy show which was kind of satirical and involved having a go at politicians, my background could be useful, would I be interested in working on something like that? I jumped for joy – this was it, my break, and it had only taken a serious cocaine and alcohol addiction to secure it. The Lord did indeed move in mysterious ways. I said that I'd love to and he suggested that we meet up when we were all out and he would tell me more about it and we could work out exactly what it was that I could do on the show. We all rolled back to The Priory and snuck back in through my window.

I told Oaksey the next day that I thought I had got a job in TV. He congratulated me and told me that, as long as I was careful, this was the break I had been looking for. Maybe soon I would be earning the £100,000 that I'd lied to Ludmilla about.

'You've certainly got an incentive now with the credit

card bills,' he laughed. 'She won't be living in your current place for long – she's an ambitious girl. You'd better get yourself a big country pad that'll keep her happy.' Oaksey laughed again; it was unnervingly difficult to know when he was joking.

I went to say goodbye to DLT and Cliff. I caught them right at the end of a chat session. There was a new intake, including some politician that I'd never heard of, a young Tory of the new school. He couldn't stop himself from goosing older women. While not a problem in his constituency where it apparently helped him get the nomination, it was causing problems in the Commons with some of the Blair Babes. I was going to miss this place. It was like living in a *News of the World* editorial meeting where they constantly discussed the stories that they couldn't print. Sir Cliff and DLT wished me the best of luck and Cliff invited me to a charity table-tennis event he was hosting in a couple of months.

'I'm doing a couple of numbers as well in the evening, it should be a lot of fun, uuh-uh.' I stayed non-committal and bade them goodbye. That night Arthur visited me for the first time since I'd been in The Priory.

'Think you're the dog's bollocks now, do you? Think you're all sorted and don't need old Arthur, huh? We'll see. You'll come crawling back to me when it all goes fuck-shaped, you wait and see, you little shithead.' He was really angry. Maybe I had made more progress than I had realised. It felt good though. I hadn't told Oaksey about Arthur but he was definitely trouble and life was better when he wasn't around. Maybe I wasn't better, here I was reasoning with myself about a talking dog that continually turned up in my head and made me do the wrong things. On the other hand the dog was visiting me less and was now angry with me for a different reason so maybe it was a good thing. Maybe everyone has an angry talking dog that comes along and gives you aggressive advice. I wasn't sure. Therapy fucks with your head.

Ludmilla picked me up the next morning. I didn't actually know that she could drive so it was a nice surprise. Five minutes down the road, I realised that she couldn't. Oblivious to the danger she was placing both of us in, she managed to get us as far as Kensington High Street without mishap. Then she ploughed headlong into a man on a Harley Davidson, sending the 'Oooh Gary Davis' wannabee flying over the handlebars. Once he'd picked himself up, he clearly saw it as his bikerly duty to take his aggression out on the hapless boyfriend of the driver and proceeded to drag me from the car and repeatedly smash me over the head with his helmet until I lost consciousness. There was a curious synergy about the whole thing. I had gone into The Priory as a result of a beating and so it kind of made sense that I was welcomed back into the real world with another one.

Ludmilla and I hobbled off into the nearest pub. I downed a couple of pints and a tequila shot and felt a bit better. Ludmilla was drinking bourbon on the rocks. I had no idea why. She normally drank beer. I wondered whether she had another boyfriend. I downed another beer. This was not the time to rock the boat.

All Must Have Prizes

IT TOOK ME a couple of weeks to ring the TV producer. Once out of The Priory, it was actually quite difficult to adjust. Things that Oaksey had told me kept bouncing round my head and I realised that I had grown quite used to the City lifestyle, however unhealthy it had been. Just doing nothing freaked me out a bit. I'd get up in the morning late – about eleven – and feel guilty, a hangover from the Protestant work ethic of boarding school. Late risers were losers. I'd then spend most of the day wandering around Portobello waiting for something to happen.

I'd walk down Westbourne Park Road, left on to Kensington Park Road, wave at my dry cleaners, turn left on to Elgin Crescent, wave at Ben in Mr Christian's then left again on to Portobello Road, avoid the market trader with the scar who'd hit me when I refused to move my Vespa from some spot he claimed he owned, pop into shoe shop, why? I don't need shoes. Up to Coffee Republic, not Starbucks, they're evil like McDonald's. Why? I didn't know. They just are. That's the way it is. On past tacky Indian shop under the Westway, wander around the farmer's market watching their last-ditch attempts to stave off suicide by charging twenty pounds for a courgette. On and on it went.

After a couple of weeks of this I realised that I had to get things moving. I rang one of the producers who was just out himself. He sounded happy to hear from me and invited me to a big bash in Soho that he was having to celebrate his release. I walked into the trendy Soho bar at a quarter past seven. It was heaving. The room was packed with well-known faces and everyone was already well on their way to being shitfaced. I hadn't quite realised how powerful and well connected the producer guy was. I had clearly chosen well. Downstairs about five table-tennis tables were set up. Everyone got organised into foursomes and the games commenced. I was soon to learn that table tennis was the real celebrity vice of choice. It was incredibly popular with anyone who'd been in The Priory, and that meant most people. If you played table tennis then networking was a much easier business.

I ordered a double vodka and cranberry, my usual kickstarter. I had made a decision that I was not going to become one of those post-therapy vegan types. I was going to drink when I wanted to but stay off the cocaine. It looked like everyone else had decided the same thing apart from the keeping off the cocaine bit. After a couple of minutes the producer guy spotted me and, totally pissed, came over to give me a big media hug. He slobbered something in my ear and then wandered off to a group of girls in minuscule clothes standing by his table-tennis table. I didn't get to talk to him for about another hour. I finally cornered him as he was waiting at the bar.

'Great party, thanks for asking me,' I shouted over the din.

'Yeah, baby, no problem. Two whisky sours please!' he screamed at the barman.

'Listen, I'd like to chat about that job.'

'What job?' He looked perplexed.

'The satire show thing, where you could use my political knowledge?' I continued.

'Oh . . . that's gone away, didn't get commissioned. I'm doing a makeover show now, some City fuck's flat gets a woman's touch. It's shit but big bucks, little work. Satire's crap, too intellectual. I might get a series out of this and then we've got a gardening thing going where we get celebrity gardeners to turn some Watutsi warrior's garden in Kenya into a typical Cotswold-type thing, it's brilliant.' He wandered off with his drinks towards a pneumatically breasted Amazonian who had definitely become his main interest of the evening.

I was pissed off and about to leave when a voice asked me whether I wanted a drink. I turned round to see a very well-known weatherman, slightly pissed, with a big smile on his face.

'I couldn't help overhearing your conversation there. Looks like you've received your first TV brush-off. Don't take it to heart. People promise lots of things in this biz – they just love to please people until they actually have to do something about it. What are you drinking?' He waved at the barman. I liked him immediately. He was cooler than he appeared on TV, though it would have been difficult not to be unless he was flatlining. 'Are you trying to get into telly generally or are you fixed on entertainment?' he asked.

'I did a bit of politics but I think that I'd like entertainment but I don't really know where to start. Ideally I'd like to work on something and have a look at how it works and then decide what it is that interests me.' I felt a little drunk but happier now someone was listening to me.

'I presume you don't want to get into the whole weather scene but I do know quite a few people in entertainment, I'll have a look around for you.' He downed a large vodka tonic in one gulp.

'Thanks,' I stammered. 'I couldn't do weather anyway, aren't you guys all trained barometers . . . I mean meteorites or whatever?' I really was a bit pissed.

'Oh no, most of us are unemployed actors. They take you and give you a crash course at this place in Hanley and then, Bang, you're on telly – it's not exactly rocket science. You just go rainy here, sunny there, low pressure, high pressure, it's all bollocks and no one expects you to get it right.' He laughed to himself and downed another vodka and tonic. He seemed to have the constitution of an ox. 'Tell you what, I only live round the corner, why don't you pop back with me and I'll take down your details and give you a couple of numbers to try tomorrow. How does that sound?' He smiled a bit oddly at me.

'That's fine, great, thanks a lot, that would be brilliant.' At least I'd get something out of this party, I thought. I wasn't going to meet anyone else, as everyone was off their tits. The marching powder had made its appearance and it was obvious that the producer had just indulged as he was sweating profusely and gibbering on to the Amazonian about how she would make a great gardener. Time to go, I thought.

We left the bar and wandered down Wardour Street towards Shaftesbury Avenue. 'What's the weather going to be like tomorrow?' I laughed but he didn't say anything. I guessed that it wasn't that original a joke. We turned down a little alley and into the entrance of a small mansion block. The building had clearly been quite grand once but it had been left to rot for quite a while. The place was damp and carpets were curling up at the corners. By his front door there was a dead yucca plant. He opened the door and ushered me in. The flat was nice in a rather dull way. If Loyd Grossman had looked round it for *Through the Keyhole* then you wouldn't have taken long to guess that it might be a weatherman living there.

'Nice place, do you live here on your own, are you married?' I asked innocently.

He chuckled to himself. 'No, I'm not married, do you want a drink?'

'Uh, a beer or something would be fine.' We were in the sitting room and I sat down on a slightly dowdy sofa. Something moved and I jumped up. A sniffly Pekinese scuttled off the sofa and ran towards my host.

'Oh, I see that you've met Typhoon.' He picked the dog up.

'Do you like music?' he continued.

'Yes, what have you got?' I replied, not really caring. I should get these numbers and go home, I was really too pissed. He went over to the corner where he had an old gramophone on a small table. I'd seen it and assumed that it was for decoration but he turned it on and chose a 78 from a stack on the floor. 'A Nightingale Sings on Berkeley Square' wafted through the air and he started waltzing around the room clutching Typhoon tightly to his chest. He began to sing along. I pushed myself back into the sofa and started to plan an exit strategy. When the song finished I asked him where his loo was. 'Just down the hall on the left.' He put on another 78 and started dancing with Typhoon again. I went into the loo and locked the door behind me.

I sat and tried to work out how to get out as quickly as possible with the numbers that I needed. I looked around the room. The walls were covered in photos. Mostly of my host in leather pants hanging out with what looked like The Village People. Bizarrely, in pride of place on the door was a picture of what looked like him meeting the Pope. This was the only photo in which he wasn't in some form of rubber Lederhosen. I suddenly clicked that there might be an alternative scenario going on here, a hidden agenda that I hadn't really picked up on. I had to leave. I would make my excuses and leave, now. I unlocked the door and made my way back into the living room. The weather presenter was stark bollock naked in the middle of the room. There was no sign of Typhoon, just the huge erection that he was sporting and the sound of men grunting from a rather graphic porno flick on the small telly in the corner. I froze. Things happened in a blur. With remarkable force he grabbed hold of me and pushed me down on to the sofa.

'My forecast is that things are going to get a bit turbulent,' he whispered before sticking his tongue in my ear. I tried to resist but he was surprisingly strong and he started ripping my clothes off. Out of the corner of my eye I could see Typhoon. He was sitting in the corner of the room behind the telly just watching. I don't know exactly what I was expecting him to do but it was really creepy. I won't go into the details of what happened to me that night but suffice to say that there was none of the tenderness that El-Bubba had shown me in Morocco. This was brutal, primal rape. I kept shouting 'No' but to no avail. He knew what he wanted and he took it with little regard for me. I felt numb, in shock; I switched off after a while and let him do what he wanted. There was no use resisting. He had the strength of ten men. When it was over I lay on the sofa in considerable pain. He got up and left the room. After about five minutes I got up and started to put my clothes on. He suddenly came back into the room and looked at me in total disgust.

'Get out, you fucking whore,' he shouted at me. I remember thinking that he must have looked at his papal souvenir and Catholic guilt must have kicked in. I picked up my shoes and ran out of the flat, down the stairs and into the street. I fell to the ground and started weeping, the sobs shaking my whole body. It was raining and I sat there until I was soaking wet, trying to cleanse myself in the freezing downpour. Eventually I got up and walked home. It took me two hours and I had to get Ludmilla to open the door as I'd lost my keys. She looked at me in an accusing manner but I just walked past her, got into the shower and scrubbed myself clean. I got into bed and didn't get out of it for twenty-four hours. When I finally did get up I realised that I had been literally shafted by the TV industry before I'd even got started.

(Oaksey says that this was definitely the turning point in my life. I could either take it lying down, so to speak, or fight back. To me, that morning, there was no question of what I had to do. The worm had turned, I'd had enough of loserdom. I was going to take control, fight back, succeed.)

I got hold of Max Clifford's telephone number from Directory Enquiries. I rang up and got the address from the receptionist. An hour later I was in his office. I had no intention of using his services as official purveyor of celebrity muck to the tabloids but I knew that his very name sent shivers down the spines of publicity-shy celebs. I just needed some proof that I was in contact with him, something to scare the weatherman with. After about half an hour I was given ten minutes with Clifford. I made up some story about how I had something juicy on a Tory MP. There was nothing he liked better than Tory bashing, even now Blair was in power. I told him that it was of a compromising sexual nature and that I didn't want to reveal anything just yet but wanted to know my options. He talked me through various things including exclusives with tabloids, a no-holds-barred confessional TV interview with someone lightweight and even, if there was enough of a story, a book deal. I told him that I'd think about it and asked for a card and contact numbers from him. I got a couple of business cards and managed to nick a couple of sheets of blank paper with his letterhead on it as I went through his reception.

Two days later, the weatherman's agent, a surprisingly influential one considering his position, received a letter from Max Clifford announcing that his client, a Mr Joly, had retained his services in regard to a story about how his client had brutally raped his client. He had several news-papers on stand-by and was keen to run the story this weekend but he just wondered if the weatherman wanted the chance to settle out of court, so to speak. I put my mobile number on the top of the letter and said that if he had an offer then it should be made within the next four hours or we would assume that he was happy for it to go to the papers. I hand delivered the letter and went to sit in the nearest coffee shop to wait. Half an hour later, my phone rang. I'd landed the big one.

I met the agent in Patisserie Valerie on Old Compton

Street. It felt right somehow. We sat at the back in a booth, the agent looked very hassled. I felt completely calm, in control. The agent started off: 'OK, you've got us over a barrel. My client made a terrible mistake. He assures me that it was all a misunderstanding and that he meant you no harm. What has happened has happened. We obviously would rather that this didn't become public knowledge so we are prepared to make a significant financial offer if we can just put all this behind us, so to speak.' He looked nervous, this clearly wasn't the sort of negotiating that he was used to.

'I don't want money.' I smiled at him, trying to look enigmatic. I was quite enjoying this.

'Well, what do you want?' The agent looked even more worried now, he was clearly faced with a lunatic.

'I want a fucking career, I want something that I can do in television, I don't want to fuck around as a runner making fucking tea for a bunch of fuckers. I want to have a TV programme, something that is mine, that I can make a name on, I need the fucking break that only happens to people who are fucking connected to fucking people like you.' I was using fuck a lot, it made me feel like I sounded hard.

The agent sat staring at me for a while, clearly thinking through his options. Most likely he was thinking about whether he should call the police and dump the weather forecaster. There were plenty more where he came from. But the British public grew strangely attached to their weather forecasters. They become little cult figures and it takes quite some time before they can get to a certain level. With supermarket openings and game-show appearances, as well as random spin-off articles and radio shows, he was a nice little earner for the agent who, facing the new influx of reality TV contestants, was not doing quite as well as he used to. I could see all this going on in his head and I let him stew in it for a while.

'Do you want to go on a couple of game shows, win some money, that sort of thing? I could probably get you on one or two but then it would be up to you.'

I snorted in derision. 'I want my own show, something that is my fucking breadwinner, something I can be linked with, get ads off, have a public face from, I want to be a fucking celebrity. I want to be somebody, I'm sick of being nobody.' I realised that this was actually true. This was better than therapy.

The agent rocked back in his seat again; he was thinking but he had a look on his face that seemed to indicate that he had an idea. He gulped his coffee, slammed the cup down into the saucer and sighed.

'OK, I think I've got what you're after but it's not going to be easy. I've got these two kids who've come in with a great idea for a show, it's a kind of revamped *Candid Camera*. It's difficult to explain but it's got legs and the ideas are strong. The keynote gag is a guy shouting into a huge mobile phone in various places. It feels right, it's very now, it's perfect for Channel 4. The problem is that these kids are passionate about it, see it as their baby.' He hesitated.

'Just fucking pay them off, it sounds great. How hard can that be for fuck's sake?' I liked the sound of this.

'It'll cost a bit – they came to us with the thing and they'll be very protective over it.'

'Up to you, but I reckon being bum-raped by a weather

forecaster is gonna cost you quite a bit as well but we could have a go and see which is the most expensive . . .' I smiled at him.

'Let me sort it out. I'll tell them that Channel 4 want to do it but want to put their own person in. Enough money will swing it. Only problem is, can you do this thing? It means that you'll be the on-screen talent and Channel 4 will need to know that you can do it. They're not going to take a punt on a complete unknown.' He looked worried.

I looked at him confidently. 'I've got a couple of friends in high places who could press some buttons with Channel 4. I'm sure that they'll agree, don't worry about it.' I tried to remember if I still had Mandy's phone number. A call from me would be the last thing he needed and he should be able to do something to keep me out of the way.

'You'll need representation, of course,' smiled the agent.

'Of course, got anyone in mind?' I smiled back. At last I was in business.

Naked and Famous

A MONTH AND a half later *Trigger Happy TV* was commissioned by Channel 4. I was really thrown in at the deep end but found that I had finally wandered into something I was actually good at. The job meant I had to lie and annoy perfect strangers. I had seen programmes like *Candid Camera* when I was a kid and they had sometimes made me laugh. To me, the funny aspect was introducing a little bit of surrealism into someone's day. I was never very excited by the *Candid Camera* type 'reveal' where people were shown the cameras and expected to laugh along with the joke. To me the real humour lay in imagining what they were thinking about. I liked picturing the scene at their homes that evening where they tried to explain to their wives that they had been accosted by a scout asking them to help him get his Greco-Roman wrestling badge. I could almost see the wife shaking her head, presuming that he had been on the bottle all day. It took a year to make and was harder than I originally thought but the ideas were strong and, by trial and error, we managed to put together six half-hours.

To celebrate, Ludmilla and I decided to get married and we had a gorgeous wedding at Tooting Bec town hall. I left Ludmilla to do the invitations and so sadly no one turned up, but we enjoyed the day nevertheless. We had no time for a honeymoon as I went straight back to work.

The job certainly had its weird moments – I had a can of baked beans thrown at me in a supermarket by a nun who thought that I was accusing her of shoplifting, to this day the most violent reaction I've received. Then there was the time I was arrested by the Zermatt snow patrol for scaring skiers whilst dressed as a yeti. I spent seven hours in the ski resort's only prison cell with what I assumed must be the only burglar in town. He was pretty nervous about my costume and thought that I was being used by the police to extract information about him. The entire team spent the best part of a year driving around the UK and Europe in a Toyota Previa as a sort of prankster A Team. Getting the big mobile phone through customs was always a bit of a problem especially when we went to the USA. The customs man actually asked me to turn the thing on to prove that it worked. When the series took off, I started getting invited to big showbiz events and I once suffered the indignity of standing in the artists' queue to get into the Brits and having the security men spend ages examining the big mobile in front of a bemused Lou Reed. I was doing a 'turn' in the show but it was not how I'd always imagined meeting the great man. Ludmilla really didn't have a clue what was happening. I would come home late straight from shoots wearing a chicken outfit or dressed as a woman and she would just laugh and carry on watching telly. She had acquired quite a strange Texan accent and was totally obsessed with all matters petroleum. It was only when I came home one afternoon to catch her watching *Dallas* that I realised what was happening. She was obsessed by the show and was clearly picking up her English from it. If we were to ever have a conversation on the oil business, it would have been fairly fluent. As it was, a typical conversation would go something like this:

Her: Howdy, DJ, whatya'll hoed up for? We got us a brunch at Cliff and Crystal's tonight.

Me: What the fuck are you talking about, brunch is a mixture of lunch and breakfast and it's six thirty in the evening and who the hell are Cliff and Crystal?

Her: Have you been drinking again? If only Jock were still around, he'd knock some sense into your goddamn head.

Me: This is a fucking lunatic asylum, who the fuck is Jock?

Her: I'm your goddamn wife, DJ. I got needs and if you don't satisfy me then I'm gonna go get me some goddamn oil jockey to ride mamma.

Me: You're off your rocker, I'm off to the pub. I'm trying to make a TV show, not live in one.

Her: I'm your goddamn wife, DJ, I got needs, I'm going crazy hanging around this ranch all day with nothing to do.

Me: I'm going to the pub.

Once I cracked the code, everything made more sense. It didn't really help us communicate but at least I knew what she was talking about. The problem was that I was never certain whether she was just reiterating storylines that she'd heard or whether she was actually trying to tell me something. I don't think I ever really worked that one out.

We delivered *Trigger Happy TV* on 5th September, 1999. I didn't really think that it would be a big hit but was just happy that I'd made a programme and could hopefully carry on working in telly. I had plans to try and make some sort of documentary next but the show was an enormous hit and I was caught up in the vortex. I began to get recognised on the street. I was a bit wary of being recognised as a prankster. I remembered seeing Jeremy Beadle once in a pub in Highgate. It was at the height of his first success, *Game For a Laugh,* where he and three other oddities played pranks on the public. On this particular evening, Beadle was just leaving the bar with two pints of beer tucked into his good arm. A rather aggressive-looking man stood up in front of him and asked him whether he was game for a laugh. To be fair to Beadle there was very little he could do but to say that yes, he was game for a laugh. The aggressive man proceeded to pour a pint of beer all over the hapless presenter. The whole pub roared with laughter; there was definitely an undercurrent of mob revenge. I was going to have to be very careful.

I remember my very first autograph request. I was standing in WH Smith's on Notting Hill Gate, flicking through a copy of *Big-Breasted Asian Babes,* whiling away the time before the pubs opened. As I was admiring the unique talents of Indira, 52-44-50, someone sidled up next to me. He was a short little runt of a man and at first I thought that he might be in need of some help to get something off the top shelf. It turned out that he was after an autograph as he loved the show. At that moment I realised that I had lost a very precious asset that you only really appreciate when it's gone: the ability to read pornography in public without people saying: 'Oh, look, there's that bloke with the big phone off the telly reading a porn mag, HELLO, I'M IN A SHOP LOOKING AT PORN MAGS!!! Look,

Mummy, it is him. HELLO . . .' Anyway I had to sign my first autograph ever on Indira's voluptuous left breast. He seemed perfectly happy but then everyone in the shop started looking at me and I had to put *Big-Breasted Asian Babes* back on the shelf and pick out something else like the *Spectator* so that it looked like I really was browsing and hadn't just come in there to read *Big-Breasted Asian Babes*.

The whole autograph syndrome is a weird one. I can understand the people who have proper autograph books and end up giving their grandchildren a book containing the signatures of The Beatles, Elvis Presley and Cary Grant. That's probably worthwhile. I also sort of understand the people who hang about outside studios and gigs and get famous musicians to sign electric guitars and stuff. They can sell this on eBay so at least they are making money out of it. The truly freakish ones are the random autograph requesters. They suddenly spot you in the supermarket and ask you to sign something like a till receipt. What do they do with it? I know that when I was at prep school in Oxford, I would hang around the parks (no, not like that) and watch Oxford University play all the county sides. At the end of the match I would run on to the pitch and get the autographs of people like Ian Botham or Geoff Boycott. I would get them to scrawl their names on scraps of paper that I would then shove into my pocket to take out and stare at for the next couple of hours. By the evening I would have lost them or thrown them away. I loved the adrenaline of meeting the cricketers but never really knew why I got their autographs. Maybe it was a form of trophy, physical proof that you'd had an encounter with the famous person. Possibly it was a meeting ritual. It gave you something to ask for and was something for them to do. It allowed you to have someone's attention for a minute or so without having to bore them to death with your views on the LBW laws. I always tried to give someone an autograph, whatever the circumstances, and always tried to write their names and something personal on it even if it was 'fuck off'. I remember reading about Steve Martin. He had a load of cards printed up that read:

Steve Martin

Actor and Comedian

This is to certify that you had a personal interactive meeting with myself and that you found me to be charming, amusing and sexy.

He would sign these cards and hand them out to eager fans. I loved the idea, it was slightly ironic, it was funny and it gave people something worth keeping. For some reason that I now forget, I found myself at Geneva airport with two hours to kill. Autographs were very much on my mind because it was in this very airport, many years before, that I'd seen David Bowie eating a hotdog. I kid you not. I was such a Bowie fan and took ages trying to pluck up the courage to go up to him and say hello. I went through all kinds of agonies as I tried to think of some cool thing to say that no one else would have ever said. The best that I could come up with was 'Would you consider *Diamond Dogs* to be a concept album or do you simply see it as the final chapter of a Ziggy trilogy?' I went through it in my head for some time but eventually realised that I sounded like a Marillion fan. I walked off and have regretted it to this day. I should have just sauntered up and said: 'Hey, Dave, how are the hotdogs?' He might have said something like: 'They're OK, thank you. Would you like to come back to my Swiss rock mansion and jam?' I could then have replied with something like: 'Thanks, David, I'd love to but I'm really busy, maybe some other time.' He would have looked dumbfounded and I could then have walked away complimenting him on his new teeth. Or maybe not, but I still think about it. Anyway I was in Geneva airport and there was this electronic (as opposed to clockwork) machine that printed personalised greetings cards. I got to work and ended up with the following:

Dom Joly

Comedian

**This is to certify that you met me
and thought I was brilliant.
I liked you too.**

I thought this was quite cool and for five Swiss francs I got a stack of thirty. I put them in my wallet and promptly forgot about them. About six months later, I was in a pub when this lovely-looking girl came up and asked me for my autograph. She claimed that it was for her brother and that he was a big fan, but I knew her game. I suddenly remembered the cards and took one out of my wallet, signing it with a flourish. I handed the card over to the girl and sat back waiting for a laugh. Unfortunately she looked at it as though I'd handed her a piece of used bog roll. She tore the card up and walked off calling me 'a pompous little prick' as she sashayed over to some scary-looking traveller type in the corner who started looking at me in a very threatening manner. I guess you have to be Steve Martin to get away with that kind of stuff.

Other weird things started to happen. When you bumped

into another 'celebrity' or bloke off the telly you instantly nodded at each other like you were in some club that you hadn't realised you'd joined. It's a bit like when you drive a Vespa and you stop at the traffic lights. If another Vespa drives up, he nods at you as though you are somehow in it together. It doesn't matter that I might be riding a cool, vintage Vespa and that he could be a convicted paedophile with halitosis on one of those hideous new hairdryer models. To him we're together forever, us against the world. I fucking hate it, that's why I put a sticker on my Vespa that says, 'Vespas are for cunts'. This always confuses them. The only people who wave at me now are the sort I'd probably get on with. It's the same in the celeb world. I tried to be a bit ironic at the beginning and started wearing a T-shirt that said 'no eye contact please' whenever I went to any glitzy function. The problem was that people thought it was funny whereas I actually meant it, so that didn't work. As a famous face the conversation you have with another famous face that you've never met before goes a bit like this:

Celeb: All right?

Me: Yeah, you?

Celeb: Yeah, this thing's really boring but I had to come . . . you know . . . show my face.

Me: Yeah, me too, I'm off in a minute.

Long pause while we both look bored.

Celeb: I really liked your stuff, really good.

Me: Thanks, I love your stuff too, really great.

Celeb: You should come down to the house one weekend, Damien lives next door, always popping in.

Me: Yeah, cool, where's your house?

Celeb: Marrakesh.
Me: Cool.
Another long pause
Me: Who's Damien?
Celeb: Damien . . . Damien Hirst.
Me: Oh yeah . . . Damien.
Celeb: Do you want a line?
Me: Normally I'd love to but, big day tomorrow . . .
stuff . . . you know?
Celeb: Yeah, totally. I don't think I'll do any tonight,
I'm right in the middle of stuff.
Me: Cool.
Celeb: I've got to rock.
Me: What?
Celeb: I'm off.
Me: Oh yeah . . . cool.

Introductions are never made. No one ever actually mentions anything by name so that, if you don't know what the person has just done or is up to or there was a big turkey, everyone's on safe ground. The whole C list, B list thing is never talked about. To a London celeb it's all about how many removals you are from Madonna. If you have meals with her then you're A list. Otherwise, frankly, you're a fuckwit. The problem is that everyone knows that they're a fuckwit but hopes that somehow things might change if they go to enough celeb bashes. By getting in enough magazines and getting enough 'face time' then maybe things might change and you get the right gig and Madonna sees/hears it and invites you over and then you can shit on all the other fuckwits that you despise so much. I don't know what people did before Madonna came to England.

Now everything is so simple. I have never dined with Madonna. I am a fuckwit. Maybe this book will change that. Somehow I doubt it. But if you are reading this, Madge, I can't do Tuesday evenings – Narcotics Anonymous – you know how it is. Oh and I'm a macrobiotic, which I think you used to be but might not be any more, I can't remember. Also I don't want to come if Trudi Styler and Sting are there. It's not that I'm being picky but I think it would be awkward since Sting and I don't get on. I've never met him but I've seen him in interviews and I just think that it's probably a no-no. Also if you're still with Guy Ritchie then it's probably best that you and I meet up somewhere without him as I know someone who knows someone who knew him who thinks he's an arse. I might get a bit drunk and then blurt it out and then we'd have a fight and he'd start crying like a baby and you'd lose respect for him and leave him and it would all be my fault. I'm being picky now. Let's just see what happens.

You try to stay sane when faced with offers of massive amounts of money, more than what you used to earn in a year to do something soul-destroying. One of the first corporate offers I got was to 'do' the big mobile thing at Vodaphone's Earls Court office party. I agreed and turned up thinking that I would be the only 'performer' only to find myself with a trailer in a row of trailers with people like All Saints and Kid Creole and the Coconuts waiting for their turn to suck the devil's cock. There exists a kind of weird underground circuit of corporate gigs where 'artists' can do their thing, earn lots of money and no one has to know about it (well, apart from the three thousand-odd Vodaphone employees at the event). I was certainly proud when my moment came and I had to introduce the chairman of Vodaphone: 'HELLO, NO, I'M AT THE VODAPHONE OFFICE PARTY AND HERE'S CHRIS GENT, THE CHAIRMAN. NO, HE'S GREAT. CIAO.' Frankly, money for old rope. I took the money and had a suit hand-made for me by Richard James in Savile Row, so can't complain.

Then there were the everyday problems of being labelled a prankster that you don't really think about. Try getting a pizza delivered or even buying something in a shop when you're a TV prankster. My doorbell would go, and I would open the door to the pizza delivery man only to have him shout from inside his helmet that I would never catch him out as he hurled the pizza at me and got back on his bike giving me the bird. Shop assistants refuse to believe that you might actually have some down time from TV in which you need to buy something. I would approach a till with something I intended to purchase only for the shop assistant to shout: 'Cunt, cunt, cunt, cunty cunt. Now try and use that on your fucking show. Where are the cameras? You'll never catch me out, is it behind the mirror, is it? Is it?' I'd eventually slip out of the shop empty-handed, leaving the assistant trying to prise the mirror off the wall to find the hidden cameras. Cab drivers would pick me up and drive me ten miles out of my way and drop me off whilst telling me that he was very sorry but he was a stupid cab and there was nothing he could do about it.

It certainly opened up opportunities that I'd never dreamt of. Suddenly I was the voice of Branston Pickle or was advertising British Airways even though they'd never upgraded me once, which used to piss me off. I remember being at the airport in the Bahamas trying to persuade the sour-faced person behind the check-in desk that I was worthy of an upgrade whilst Michael Caine calmly waited for me to finish before cruising through to first class. On arrival at Heathrow, I was shoved out of the way, at the luggage belt, by some special services woman who couldn't quite get far enough up Michael's bottom. I bet he's had supper with Madonna.

One day someone from an American film company rang me. Had I ever thought of writing a film? Would I like to come in for a meeting? For some reason I love meetings so I always say yes to them. I think I love them because they are the closest that my job gets to a normal type existence. Everyone understands meetings – you go to a nice office, talk bollocks, get a free coffee and you don't actually have to do anything there and then. But these film meetings became quite surreal. The first time I went, there were three exec types who went on for half an hour about how they loved the whole *Trigger Happy* thing and did I have any ideas for a film? After so much sycophancy you feel obliged to come up with something to prove your worth. I'd never even thought about a film and had no real interest in it. I'd always preferred TV. But in this kind of meeting you'd eventually find yourself saying something like:

Me: I've always thought *National Lampoon's European Vacation* was funny. That's probably the kind of film that I'd like to do if I ever did one.
Them: OK, I like it, so it's a kind of road movie type thing, that's good, loads of different iconic UK settings, good cameo potential. Forget the *Lampoon* thing, Chevy Chase is a fucking arsehole – trust me, I've met some arseholes and he's king sphincter. Kicked me off a studio jet once so that his fucking Chihuahua could have a fucking seat to go and see a fucking Nicks game. He's

fucking dumptruck big time, forget about him.

Me: Maybe it's on a tour bus or something?

Them: That's it, *The Tour Guide*, you're the tour guide and we get lots of Famous American actors and they go round the country with you and funny things happen on the way. It's like *Airplane* on a bus. What kind of things do you see happening?

Me: Uuhhmm . . . well, maybe we see the Loch Ness Monster?

Them: Oh YES, BABY, spoof horror, very sexy, maybe there's a girl and you save her without knowing but she thinks you do and we could have druids or something.

Me: Uuhm . . . yeah, something like that.

Them: I think we could green light this fucker straight away. How long would you take to write it? We are very excited about this project.

Me: Write it? I thought you guys would write it. Uuhhmm, maybe six months? I have no idea. I mean there's not actually really an idea here and I don't even write letters so a film might take some time. Maybe five years? Two years? I have no idea.

Them: You've got yourself a fucking deal, kid. How about twenty grand up front? You give us a script in six months, we'll get on to agents and sound out who's around. This is fucking exciting.

Other them: We are really excited by this.

Other other them: This is going to be hot, this is really exciting.

A month later we had another meeting:

Other: Green fucking lights all the way down the fucking boulevard, baby. They fucking love it and apparently Jack Black, you know him, he's seen *Trigger Happy* and he's on board with whatever you do, he thinks you rock.

Me: What have they actually green lit?

Other: They've green lit *The Tour Guide* except they want to call it *The Big Guy* – that's you.

Me: But we don't even have a story, we were just riffing I thought?

Other: They are confident enough in the initial scenario to green light the whole damm thing, it's very exciting.

Me: They've green lit the riff?

Other: Damn fucking right they have and they're thinking about Kate Beckinsale for the woman of the lake.

Me: What woman, what lake?

Other: The fucking maiden of the lake . . . loch whatever it is that you save from the Lake Ness creature, like in King Kong.

Me: I think this might all be going a bit fast, I'm doing a new series and I'm busy and I would want to give this my full attention so maybe we can hold back for a while.

Other: If it's money let me talk to your agent – we'll see you happy. We're all very excited.

Me: I'm going to go now, I'm late for something . . .

This went on for about six months with me unable to resist a meeting, listening to them get more and more excited about my movie that they had made up. Almost exactly six months after the first meeting I got a call from one of the exec's assistants.

Assistant: Hey, is that Don Jelly?

Me: Dom Joly, yeah. Who's this?

Assistant: I'm Brad, I work in Tony Monka's office.

Me: Hey Brad, what's happening, time for another meeting?

Assistant: Hey listen, I'm just the messenger. Tony wanted me to ring you personally to let you know that we just got a red light, he's really sorry, he can't understand what happened but it's a definite red light.

Me: What had been red lit and does that mean whatever it is is cancelled?

Assistant: Don't get hassled with me, man, I'm just the messenger, they've red lit *If It's Tuesday This Must Be Scotland*.

Me: I have no idea what that is, I think you must have the wrong person.

Assistant: Tony changed the name, he wanted it to be pitched more classy but Jack Black is doing the Ali G movie now, says that he fucking loves the script, very cool, so the whole thing is red lit.

Me: So no more meetings?

Assistant: Tony says keep in touch.

And that was my movie career. It was fun while it lasted, especially as I never really wanted one in the first place. Occasionally someone from my agent's office tells me that someone has rung from LA to find out my availability to be in something that needs a fat bloke. A young Harry Secombe in the Peter Sellers story? The Pavarotti story? I'm not even an actor. God knows what would happen if something ever got off the drawing board but it always goes away. The only certainty from this business is that if something is brought up by an American, it will eventually go away. It might take some time and involve lots of meetings but it will definitely go away so don't worry about it.

Ludmilla dealt with the whole fame thing in a very different way. She saw my show when it went out as I had some friends over to watch it. It was only about halfway through that she realised that the person on telly was me. She went berserk. Television was a very big part of her life and I think that she was actually very impressed. Every week she would switch *Dallas* off and come and watch my show with me. This was high praise indeed. Then things got very weird.

We did a shoot for *Hello* in a borrowed house in Holland Park. They really wanted to do a piece on me and my home life rather than the usual merry prankster shots. I posed with Ludmilla who was given loads of clothes to try on by the stylist. She loved the whole thing and started waffling on to the stylist in her *Dallas* English. I don't know what it was but they really clicked and the stylist was laughing at everything Ludmilla said, but not in the way that I laughed at her. She almost seemed to be listening to her gibberish. Anyway, to cut a long story short, the stylist turned out to also work for someone on the *Richard and Judy* show and she obviously told someone there about Ludi. A week later, she got a call from someone asking her whether she'd like to come on the show and talk about being the other half of a TV celeb? I tried my best to explain to her what they wanted and to get her to say no. Unfortunately she got her boss to ring up and he translated a bit of what they wanted and she went mental about the idea of actually being on TV. She ended up going on the show and was an enormous hit. It was all a bit like Peter Sellers in *Being There*. She talked her usual gibberish and they lapped it up. I think they assumed that her *Dallas* talk was some sort of big metaphor for life. She was so popular that she was offered a regular job as a kind of agony aunt who answered viewers' questions in *Dallas* gobbledy-gook. I tuned in one afternoon and spent the entire show with my head in my hands.

Judy: Our next caller for Ludmilla is Janet from Leigh-On-Solent. Janet, you're through to Ludmilla.
Janet: Hello, Ludmilla. I am having real problems here as I can't seem to find a gentleman who is interested in the same sort of things as myself. A lot of the ones I meet down here are racists. How can I meet the right man?
Ludi: JR likes a lady with attitude. You murrst look real purty, do your hair right, wear something sexy and don't talk too much. Sue-Ellen would never make a man wait for her. That's just doggone rude. There's oil in them thar hills.
Janet: You think there's hope for me?
Ludi: Honey, where there's oil, there's hope.
Judy: Thanks, Janet . . . hope you got what you needed. Next up is Richard from Belsize Park . . .

She became a kind of cult figure and I would come home to find bloody Kate Moss and Stella McCartney hanging around my flat getting drunk with Ludmilla. It really pissed me off, particularly because they didn't seem to know who I was. The final insult was when I got home one night to find a note on the fridge in her worst English.

'Dom, I go to Madonna, take supper with her and Ritchie,

I late.' That was it, with all I'd bloody done and it was my wife who was supping with Madge. I got really depressed. When I saw her the next day she wouldn't tell me anything about her evening. Apparently it was, 'hush-hush, no speak about, very privacy.' Great, now even my wife had a life too important to tell me about.

I started seeing more and more of Oaksey as everything went a bit headfucky. I could afford him now whereas after I'd left the City company I had no insurance and had to stop seeing him. He seemed thrilled with my success. I think deep down he only really enjoyed doing celebs. I went to see him in his office just off Sloane Square. It was a small place for someone so apparently well connected. The walls were absolutely crammed with signed photos of celebs thanking Oaksey for his 'help' or his 'calming of stormy waters'. No one actually came out and said something like: 'Dear Oaksey, thanks for giving me loads of anti-depressants when I lost my fucking mind and had a shattering nervous breakdown. It's a shame that I now can't ejaculate but that's life, I guess. All my love, Brad Pitt.'

Things like that just never happen but he had everyone on his wall – Sean Connery, Pierce Brosnan, Dame Maggie Smith, China Crisis (China Crisis!! He could have at least done the walls in some sort of order of importance but it was clearly totally random) – there was hardly anybody up there who hadn't had supper with Madonna. I certainly wasn't up there. I wondered what the etiquette was. Did you wait for him to ask or should you just bring one in one day? It was like the signed photos you see in restaurants. My favourite restaurant in London, Bertorelli's La Toscana in Notting Hill Gate, first gave me this unique celebrity dilemma.

Firstly I love this little local restaurant because when you ring up to book they always start by saying. 'You know that we are not the famous Bertorelli's in Soho?' Anywhere that prefaces their whole business with an apology is my kind of place. They have a motley collection of signed photos on their walls ranging from Chris de Burgh and Duran Duran to, weirdly, China Crisis again, who have clearly never missed an opportunity to get their picture on any wall. The shop-keepers in the area where China Crisis lived must have dreaded another visit from the boys: 'Hey, we've got a new picture, where do you want it?' How does this work? I know for a fact that the owner of Bertorelli's La Toscana would not recognise China Crisis if the name was written in neon and plugged into their foreheads. So did China Crisis introduce themselves to Mr Bertorelli when he came to take their order? Did they hand him a signed photo produced from a small briefcase that they carried around for this very purpose? Clearly they had an efficient machine. Maybe they let their office know at the end of every week where they had been. Then a whole load of generically signed photos with things like: 'To all you guys, thanks a lot, love China Crisis' got sent off to the various establishments. I have tried to ask Signor Bertorelli but he can't remember.

Restaurants themselves become difficult things. You suddenly realise that you could get a table in places that just six months previously would have called the police if you'd turned up on their doorstep. So you experiment and ring up for a table the next day and then that evening and then ten minutes before you turn up. The Ivy is a classic example. The first time I went, Madonna was in one corner (doesn't count) and two Spice Girls in another. It was fun but by the tenth time, as you watch The Edge from U2 sitting staring at his peas in one of those 'uncomfortable couple' meals where they haven't got anything to say, you do start to wonder what the fuck you're doing there.

Then there's the celeb mag. You're too paranoid to go on holiday in case someone snaps you in your swimming trunks and you end up as part three of their fat celebs feature. There are items like 'spotted' in *Heat* where people ring up and reveal that they've seen Graham Norton walking down Carnaby Street holding an umbrella. My oddest one was when I called some idiot a 'cunt' because I turned off a main road into some country lane and nearly died when he roared out of a one-way exit. The guy's first instinct was not to book himself into some refresher driving course or stop taking mushrooms when he's driving but that this could be a story for *Heat*. He rings up and tells whoever collates these shortest of short stories what happened. Money changes when you're famous. For years you've scrimped and saved and couldn't afford anything and then, when you become famous and finally have some money, you don't have to pay for anything. If the idea appeals and you are a shameless whore there is pretty much nothing that you can't get for free. If you like a certain line of clothing, ring up their press office, pretend to be your own PA (no one who's anyone would actually ring themselves) and say that you want some clothes. They appear, as if by magic, the next day. If you want a car, then contact the dealership and say that you are thinking of getting one – the offers come flooding in. You get upgrades on flights (except BA, just my luck), free CDs sent to you before release, Play Stations coming out of your arse and all because you're on the telly. People should realise that this is the time that you *will* spend money. You *want* to spend money and flash it about. Save the free stuff for when you're over the hill, shattered from your nineteenth nervous breakdown, foaming at the mouth, living in a box under Waterloo Bridge – that's when I'll need a free Porsche.

It was at the height of all this madness that I came across the answer to the gaping holes that were appearing in my vacuous celebrity life: Kabbalah. It came at just the right time: weirdness was all around me, money was pouring in and it all just left me feeling empty and hollow like a big empty hollow thing. I'd tried the usual stuff, buying a twelve-seater hot tub and a Caribbean island but it did nothing for me. Kabbalah really changed me as a person. I guess that I was just waiting for something like it to come into my life and was ready to accept it when it came. Luckily I didn't meet Sting at that time or Ludmilla and I would have got into Tantric sex and we'd never have got anything done as we'd be too busy having thirty-six-hour orgasms and telling everyone about it. As it was, a higher power brought me to Kabbalah and for that I will be temporarily grateful. I'm still not entirely sure what it's all about but I started to wear a little bit of string on my wrist and I suddenly felt a lot better. Kabbalah deals with stuff on a really deep level, much deeper than anything I'd ever dealt with before. Oaksey was very anti it but this was my thing and I wasn't going to let anyone else put me off it. I was leaving the Life Centre in Notting Hill, having just had a three-hour karmic work out. I wandered down to Planet Organic for a glass of wheatgrass and got talking to this girl who told me all about it. She said that Lenny Kravitz had turned her on to it and it had literally changed her life. I asked her how and she did that Kabbalah thing where you can't really explain it but there's this smile that comes over someone's face and you know that it must be good. How to explain Kabbalah? Well, it deals with all the things that bother you and sorts them out very spiritually. It makes you realise that it's OK to be you and not someone else. It helps you deal with things like money and houses and shopping. It's a very ancient thing and has been handed down by ancients to wise men to celebrities. It's pointless trying to describe it to you because you're not famous but know this: it's great. I started hanging around with like-minded people that were into Kabbalah and we would spend our time in expensive coffee shops and tell each other about how happy we were and compare bracelets. In a way I feel a bit funny even mentioning it, as it is a very private thing. In fact I'm not going to go on about it any more. You've got to keep some things to yourself.

Ludmilla was starting to get more and more recognised in London and she almost had a better social life than I did. I think that I got a bit jealous and decided to do something about it. Ludmilla had always told Oaksey that she wanted to move to my country house as soon as the repairs were finished. She had been getting quite insistent about seeing it until the *Richard and Judy* gig came up. Recently she had shown no interest in leaving London as she was clearly having a whale of a time. I decided to put a stop to this new, independent Ludmilla. I was the one who should be having all the fun, not her. I had to get her out of London.

I went to my bank and checked on my royalties situation from *Trigger Happy*. It was quite healthy. I got into the car and drove out of London. I was going shopping, country house shopping.

I'm From London

I F I'M HONEST then the moving to the country idea was really about moving away from all the weirdness that had happened since the success of *Trigger Happy*. It had been a whirlwind in which I'd done and experienced an amazing amount of bizarre things but I'd had enough. I'd canned *Trigger Happy* and wasn't going to make any more. I was looking around for new ideas and needed some time to think about stuff. I just wanted to get away from everything and everyone. I'd always suffered from 'Black Dog', as Churchill called it. Although in my situation it was more 'Brown Dog' since Arthur was a brown Rhodesian Ridgeback and definitely seemed to be the physical manifestation of this condition. I felt confident that leaving London with Ludmilla was just what we needed. It was a new start, a new life and everything was going to be all right. I had never really bought anything sizeable like a house before. I wasn't entirely sure how to go about it. I'd always loathed estate agents and refused to have anything to do with them. Maybe it was something to do with my upbringing in Lebanon but they'd always seemed to be among life's great disposable objects.

If you want something, find the owner and make an offer, that's how I'd always felt. So I started to get organised. I got a map, drew a triangle emerging out of West London and drew a circle in an area approximately a hundred miles away. I then tried to dissect the circle through the line coming out of the triangle but it all got really mathematical and freaked me out a bit. I kept to the circle that was bang in the middle of the Cotswolds, which I felt was a decent enough distance to discourage commuter scum whilst still allowing me to pop into London when Ludmilla got too weird. I drove down there the next day and spent a couple of fruitless days driving round tearoom-stuffed villages, squeezing past enormous coachloads of gormless Japanese tourists cruising, lemming-like, from antique shoppe to antique shoppe. I was about to give up when I got hopelessly lost and ended up driving down a tiny country lane enclosed by thick, high hedges and a canopy of copper beech trees. It was like going down a long tunnel and I was praying for light at the end of it. Then I came round a corner and there it was, nestled under a steep hill with a thick forest on one side and a lazy river running past the other, the most beautiful house I'd ever seen. It was an enormous, thatched, two-storey ramble of a place with lovely, slightly shambolic gardens. I wanted it badly. A little sign nailed to the wooden gates told me that the name of the house was 'The Merkins'. On a second sign were handwritten the words 'For Sale'. It was too perfect. I had to have it. I pushed open the gate and walked up the path towards the large wooden door. I rang the bell and waited. I could hear footsteps inside shuffling towards the door and then a voice came through a little spyhole.

'Who is it?' enquired the voice.

'I'm from London,' I answered confidently.

'Fuck off,' said the voice with equal confidence. I've always loved the simple warmth of English country folk. They are always the first to welcome a stranger into their homes and offer them a cup of tea.

'I want to buy your house and I'm loaded,' I persisted.

There was a long silence followed by the sound of several bolts being unlocked. The door creaked open to reveal a small bald man with an unfeasibly long beard. For a second I thought that I might be tripping and that my mind had decided to take me on a behind-the-scenes tour of *The Lord of the Rings* but the hobbit spoke and he was all too human.

'Are you a cash buyer? I'll only deal in cash. I don't want to fuck around with any time wasters,' snarled the hobbit.

'I've got cash and I want your house.' I hoped that the hobbit actually did own the place.

'Did they send you? I didn't kill her, you know. She fell, she was startled by the noise. If I had wanted to kill her I would have made it more painful, I can assure you. I was in Malaya, once sliced a man in quarters with cheese wire, you don't frighten me.' The hobbit looked quite distressed. I decided to ignore the fact that he was clearly two slices short of a sandwich and plough on.

'I can pay cash, up front, but I want you out within three weeks, no estate agents, I can offer you four hundred thousand pounds, take it or leave it.'

'I'll take it,' said the hobbit and the deal was done. I hadn't even entered the house but I just knew that the place was for me. The hobbit wanted to talk more, he trusted me now and he had loads to say. 'We used to drill holes in watermelon, much better than women . . .' He was out of his mind. I just hoped that he'd be as good as his word. I drove nervously back to London, unsure of whether the deal would go through. It did, the hobbit was as good as his word and I took possession of The Merkins three weeks after I'd first laid eyes on it.

I decided to take Ludmilla down the same day. We packed

our stuff into the car and left London without so much as a glance backwards. I told Ludmilla that we were going to Southfork and I think she understood. She was in a great mood. She started singing along to Phil Collins, always a sure sign that she was happy. It was a bit annoying as I thought that I'd binned her collection but she'd clearly hidden one away and it was the worst of the lot. We cruised through places like Burford and Bibury to the sounds of a screechy East European murdering 'Sussusudio'. Old biddies looked up from their garden potterings and yellow-corded country types tut-tutted to themselves as we zoomed past. Ludmilla screamed with delight as soon as she saw The House. It was the first true moment of absolute happiness that I'd ever witnessed with her apart from when Sue-Ellen left JR. God, she had been happy that day. She rushed up the path and ran around the garden muttering to herself. We both wandered round the house. It was as gorgeous as it had seemed from the outside. We quickly unpacked our stuff and lit a big roaring fire in the drawing room. As the flames licked around the enormous old stone fireplace it began to get really hot. It was midsummer and really too hot for a fire so we had to open all the windows and then go outside into the garden to try to cool down. I decided to find our nearest pub where we could have a celebratory drink and meet the locals. I got out the map and found that our nearest village, Chipping Bottom, was only a couple of miles further on down the tunnel road. It was a gorgeous place, all Cotswold stone with not a tea shoppe in sight and a lovely old cedar tree right in the middle of the village opposite a picture-perfect little shop. For some reason the tourist coaches had missed this particular piece of old England. We parked outside the village pub, The Angry

Peasant. It was a peaceful-looking place, all tiny lead windows and a couple of old benches leaned up against the external stone wall. I decided to go in and make some new friends. I kicked the little green door and it swung open with an enormous screech that silenced the entire pub.

'Hello, country folk, I'm from London. I've just bought the big house on the hill, which makes me the new Lord of the Manor, so technically you all belong to me. Who's going to buy me a drink?' The silence in the pub was like the deepest vault of an as yet undiscovered Egyptian Pharaoh's tomb. The only sound was that of a large grandfather clock whose ticking was accentuated by the murderous silence. I peered around the room. It was packed. Groups of flat-capped, dirty-tweeded badger killers stared at me with complete hatred.

'I'm only joking . . . hello everyone. I'm Dom and this is Ludmilla and we've just moved into The Merkins . . . I'm on the telly . . .' The pub stayed totally still. I nearly backed out and left but realised that if I did I would never dare return. I walked up to the bar. I could hear my own heartbeat. 'Could I have a pint of your local bitter and a Malibu for the lady and whatever any of you good folk would like?'

The landlord looked at me for just a fraction too long before pouring me a pint and slamming it down on the bar in front of me.

'Drink up and fuck off, no one wants your sort round here,' he said, indicating the door that I had so recently given my jovial boot.

'Oh, come on, I was only joking, I'm from London, I'm sure I'll soon learn how to fit in down here. I've just moved into The Merkins up the road . . .' Before I could finish I noticed that the whole pub had looked up and were suddenly interested rather than hostile.

'You've moved into The Merkins, have you?' giggled the landlord. 'I wondered why we hadn't seen Jock in here for a while, so he finally managed to get rid of it, the lucky bastard.'

'Jock . . . Jock Ewing?' said Ludmilla, to the bemusement of the landlord.

'Ignore her, she's foreign,' I told him. 'Had he been trying to sell it for ages?' I was a bit narked as I thought that I'd done a good deal.

'Ever since the chemical plant opened upstream he was desperate to get out. Once the river was condemned, the place was never the same and he was sure that the fumes were doing his head in. The doctor said that he had less than a year to live if he didn't get out. But you know all this presumably? Very brave of you to take it on, I presume you can't have kids? Medical thing is it or is the old todger not functioning?' The landlord gave me a big leery smile.

The whole pub was smiling and listening now. I downed the pint, paid up and left before Ludmilla had even finished her Malibu. I couldn't help noticing that a lot of the pub were taking an unhealthy interest in her legs. She was wearing one of her ludicrous fake Chanel miniskirts that barely covered her bum. I'd tried to buy her some normal clothes but she had a very clear idea of how she wanted to look and that seemed to be like a Puerto-Rican hooker so there wasn't much that I could do about it. I roared back to The Merkins and went down to the river to take a closer look. It was the blackest water that I'd ever seen and there was a hint of foam in various parts of it. Most worryingly, five dead fish floated down past me as I stood there. They were belly up and bloated, their skin pock-marked as though eaten by acid. I decided that swimming was probably a no-no but felt confident that we could live with it. I dipped my finger into it and instantly pulled it out – it was boiling hot. I decided that the best thing to do was to ignore it. I went back into the house and started to unpack, everything was going to be all right. Just to be sure, I took double my dose of Prozac.

We spent the next week settling in and everything really seemed to be going well. We noticed that everyone else had dogs so, to try to fit in, we went and bought one. This old farmer woman about five miles away had put an ad in the local shop saying that she had some black Labrador puppies for sale. Black Labs were definitely the thing to have in Gloucestershire, they were everywhere. Whenever I'd driven through Chipping Bottom the village green was full of them, their owners desperately trying to work out which dog was theirs. I thought that it might be a good way to meet people and Ludmilla could have something to talk to.

The next day we drove up to Badgergas Farm to meet the old farmer woman. She looked like an extra from a zombie film and I tried not to retain eye contact as we wandered over towards one of her huge barns. She slid open the hangar-like doors to reveal a small litter of puppies feeding off their mother.

'Here they are, the little beauties, take your pick,' the mutant farmer woman said, pointing at the litter. I took a closer look and had a funny feeling that these puppies didn't look anything like black Labradors. To start with, they weren't even black.

'Are these definitely black Labradors?' I asked the mutant.

'Oh yes, they're pedigree, award-winners this lot, best in the county.'

'Why aren't they black?' I asked her nervously.

'They're never black when they're little – they become black later.'

'But why isn't the mother black then? She looks more pinkish, in fact she looks more like a pig, to be honest,' I ventured.

'Yes, well, it is a pig – the mother died and this was the next best thing, but don't worry it'll all be fine, they're great puppies. Now I hope you townies haven't come 'ere to waste my fookin' time, I've got things to do and if I don't sell these little fookers they'll 'ave to go for cow food.' She was getting quite aggressive.

'Aren't cows vegetarians?' said I.

'Vegetarians, I fookin' hate vegetarians, fookin' Communists the lot of them, traitors to their country. Of course the fookin' cow ain't a fookin' vegetarian, where do you think we are, bloody Stoke fookin' Newington? You're beginning to get on my fookin' nerves, are you foreign?' She started playing threateningly with a pitchfork and I just wanted to get out.

'My wife is, but don't worry, she's house-trained. We'll take that one,' I said, pointing at the least threatening-looking puppy. The mutant pulled it away from the pig's teat and thrust it into my arms. It had enormous teeth for a little puppy, which it immediately sank into my forearm, drawing blood.

'Right, that'll be five hundred pounds,' said the mutant, extending her dirty, long-nailed hand.

'Five hundred pounds,' I gasped. 'That's more than my car's worth.'

'This is a fookin' pedigree, townie, now pay up or fook off my land.' She started to snarl and her lips curled up into a violent expression that made me instantly reach for my wallet.

We drove out of Badgergas Farm with our little pig-dog's jaws in a deathlock on my left ankle that made changing gears quite difficult. I couldn't help thinking that I'd been ripped off but no one teaches you these things so it was difficult to know. I decided to call the pig-dog Bacon, it seemed appropriate.

He was a problem from day one. He didn't behave like any dog that I'd ever come across. He seemed to have been bred purely for aggression. He would attack absolutely anything and attack it hard. After four days of Bacon living with us, the postman threw a note into our garden saying that from now on we would have to pick up our mail from the post office as he was no longer insured to enter our garden. Apparently he had nearly lost a finger on the second day and Bacon had ripped his Achilles tendon apart on the third. The fact that we had originally bought him to make friends was laughable. On his first excursion into the village he attacked two kosher black Labradors and killed the cat that sat outside the village shop. Bacon was immediately banned from the village and the owner of one of the Labs threatened to call the police until I gave him a large wad of cash. This was not good. It would have been all right if he was a good guard dog but at night he liked to sleep on our bed and nothing would wake him up apart from us trying to get into it. He would go for us so viciously that we gave up after a couple of nights and took to sleeping in the spare room. It was just easier that way and, besides, it was on the other side of the house from the river so the fumes weren't quite so strong. All this and Bacon was only a couple of months old. I dreaded to think what he might be like when he grew up. As usual I decided to ignore the whole situation and hope that everything would sort itself out.

A month or so later I had got into the habit of taking Bacon for a walk in the forest near the house in a vain attempt to try and tire him out and lessen his aggression. It was not really a forest, more like a small wood, but I liked the idea that I was walking in a forest – it sounded better, more country, so to Bacon and me, it was a forest. Anyway, I was in the forest one morning trying to find Bacon as he'd heard a noise and had raced away from me towards the source of it. He was, no doubt, readying himself to pull apart whatever poor unsuspecting piece of wildlife had just signed its death warrant. I heard him locate his quarry as he started barking wildly. I hurried towards the sound, hoping that I might be able to get some remains of whatever he was killing for the cooking pot that night. I got to a thick wall of bushes, from behind which I could hear him in mid-struggle. I pushed back a large branch in front of me and then stood in complete shock at the scene before me.

Bacon had his little mouth clamped firmly around the left-hand claw of what looked like a chicken, a fifty-foot chicken. The thing must have been between forty-five and fifty feet at least. It was a bit like the one the French rugby team used as a mascot, with enormous feathers that hung over its claws, making it look a bit like it was wearing shoes. For some reason I've always found the concept of animals in clothes very amusing. I know it's wrong and that the PG chimps were probably ill treated and circuses are wrong when they put seals in sailor costumes but I have always had a soft spot for it. A friend of mine likes it when women burp. Don't ask me why, I know it's not right but these are the quirks that all go together to make us the complicated creatures that we are.

Anyway Bacon was in the middle of quite a hopeless fight with a fifty-foot French chicken and I was thinking about seals in costumes. I had to act. I launched myself into the clearing without any real idea of what I was going to do. I had clearly startled the enormo-chicken as it turned to face me with its frightening-looking beak raised as though about to peck. I picked up a large stick and hurled it with all my might at its head. The chicken lifted up its left leg to deflect the stick and sent Bacon flying through the air somewhere into the bushes in which I was standing. I turned and ran, with Bacon right behind me. He was in such shock that I almost felt sorry for him. I heard the chicken cock-a-doodling behind me and I ran until I thought my lungs might burst.

When I reached the house I ran inside, bolting the door as firmly as the hobbit had the very first day that I'd knocked on it. Bacon and I sank to the floor panting. Well, I did; he just dug his teeth into my arm. I like to feel that there was a touch of affection in it. I went to the kitchen and poured myself a stiff whisky before prising him off with a potato masher. Ludmilla was sitting in the ironing room watching *Knots Landing*, her new obsession, a spin-off series from *Dallas* featuring some of the minor characters.

'Hey, Ludi, guess what? Bacon just attacked a fifty-foot chicken in the forest and I had to beat him off with a stick before running back here,' I panted excitedly.

'Ray Ewing,' she replied, pointing at the telly. 'He Bobby's wife's brother,' she continued, dewy-eyed.

'Be careful going into the forest, there's a fifty-foot chicken on the loose and it looks fucking dangerous.' But she was lost to the telly and I left her to it. I had a mystery on my hands. What the hell was a fifty-foot chicken doing in the forest? Maybe there were more of them roaming the forest in giant packs picking off anything that dared enter. I checked my Prozac again, I had definitely not taken an overdose; I was on Tuesday and it was Tuesday. Maybe I'd taken a whole week's worth in my sleep? No, I had definitely seen the fucker and so had Bacon although that wasn't really going to stand up in court. The locals must all know about them, why hadn't they warned me? They were an unfriendly bunch but surely they would let you know that a herd of man-eating fifty-foot chickens were wandering around in your back yard? I felt like ringing the hobbit but couldn't face it. I opened a nice single malt and stared out of the window for a bit as I felt the whisky calm me down.

That evening I drove into Chipping Bottom and made a beeline for The Angry Peasant. I entered slightly less abruptly than the last time and there was only a brief uncomfortable silence before they all resumed chatting. Maybe I was being accepted? I ordered a pint of the frankly undrinkable local bitter, Cheddar Crucis. It was bright radioactive orange and a stranger might be forgiven for thinking that you were downing a pint of Campari. The locals drank nothing else and the local term for getting pissed was to get 'cheddared'. I had a couple of Cheddars before leaning over to the landlord, whose name, I found out, was Gerald.

'Tell me, Gerald, what sort of wildlife is to be found round here, any hunting?' I asked, trying to sound insouciant.

'Why do you ask?' said Gerald suspiciously.

I tried to play it cool. 'Oh, just because when I was taking Bacon for a walk in the forest this afternoon we came across a fifty-foot chicken and I was just wondering whether there were any others around?' The pub went completely quiet. A man near the door stood up and rammed a thick bolt on the door firmly shut.

'A fifty-foot chicken, you say,' said Gerald, trying to look lighthearted, but his eyes gave him away as they darted around the pub nervously.

'You don't want to be talking like that, people will think that you're mad as an apple. Your eyes can play tricks on you in those woods, the light through the trees and all that, artists rave about it, very deceptive it can be, very deceptive . . .'

'TELL HIM THE TRUTH, GERALD!' an old man had stood up and yelled at the landlord. 'Tell him the truth, Gerald, tell him about the giant barns. It's his right.' The old man looked around but, sensing that he didn't have the support of the pub, sat down and stared into his Cheddar as though nothing had happened.

'What barns?' I asked, looking around for help.

'Just you keep away from Badgergas Farm if you know what's good for you,' came a lone voice from the back of the pub.

'Fuck off back to London, townie,' went another.

'I am Curious Golightly, son of Mogwar,' shouted yet another man whom I took to be the village idiot. He was wearing a large, white, dirty smock, a big wide-brimmed straw hat and was chewing on a piece of straw. He certainly looked the part. Everyone told him to shut up but he had successfully changed the atmosphere and everyone lightened up a bit and returned to their drinks. I finished up quickly before walking to the door, unbolting it and stepping out into the crisp night air. As I climbed into my car I saw the village idiot leave the pub. He walked towards me and threw a piece of paper on to my front seat before disappearing into the darkness. I picked it up and unfolded it. It read:

THERE ARE LOTS OF BIG CHICKENS, THEY ARE
DANGEROUS, LEAVE HERE NOW, PS YOU HAVE
A NICE ARSE, I'M IN DANDELION COTTAGE ON
FOWLER'S HILL, NO PRESSURE.

It seemed that the village idiot was also the village homosexual. I didn't take him up on his offer but drove home in
a state of some confusion. Everyone clearly knew a lot more
about the chickens than they had let on. They obviously had
something to do with Badgergas Farm, the place where I'd
got Bacon from. I remembered that there had been extraordinarily large barns dotted around the place. Maybe the
mutant farmer woman was responsible for the mutant
chickens. Was the chemical plant anything to do with it?
Why did people worry sheep? I felt really out of my depth
in this new environment and suddenly longed for the certain-
ties of the mean streets of London. The next morning I got
up and looked out of the window to see Ludmilla pottering
about in the garden. She'd been doing a lot of pottering
about since we'd moved to the country. She seemed to actually have a knack for gardening and had started growing
vegetables. I don't know whether it was because of the
strange properties of the river but her veg patch was really
quite impressive. She had grown some oddly shaped onions
and a purple carrot thing that looked totally inedible but
that she kept putting in my omelettes. She was settling in to
country life quite well. She'd quit the *Richard and Judy* thing
and since I had begun to erase any messages from her London
friends, they had stopped ringing.

I was pleased that she had taken up a hobby like gardening.

It kept her out of trouble. Someone in the village had told me about some country fair that was happening in a couple of weeks and there was a competition on for the best vegetables. I explained the idea to her by drawing on bits of paper. It worked quite well and she seemed to understand what I was getting at and appeared keen. I met someone in the village shop who had been entering the competition for the last twenty years or so and I palmed Ludmilla on to her. They seemed to get on pretty well and this woman helped her get everything ready for the big day.

I spent more and more time in my little snug. I'd started watching loads of telly since I'd been in The Merkins. I'd become addicted to stuff like *World's Weirdest Police* and *When Giraffes Attack*. I also loved the new reality shows that were sweeping the schedules. Shows like *Touch the Truck*, where various micro-celebrities stood touching a truck until the last one passed out, were fucking genius. I had just pitched a couple of my own ideas for these kind of programmes to Channel Five and I was convinced that they were real winners. In a spin-off idea from *Touch the Truck*, I'd suggested *Touch the Goat* where five contestants had to keep physical contact with a mountain goat as it went about its day. I liked the idea of combining reality, natural history and mountain climbing and thought I might be onto a winner. I had also pitched *Stuck in a Lift With You* where a couple of celebs are trapped in a lift for three months. I thought it would give us a really interesting idea of what they were about as well as injecting a little bit of urban paranoia into the televisual landscape. I didn't really know what that meant but I had read it in a television-pitching book and it sounded good. I was eagerly awaiting replies.

Ludmilla would occasionally come up to the snug and sit with me but she hated these shows and would invariably go back downstairs for some *Knots Landing*. She must have seen every episode at least forty times but she never seemed to tire of it. At about midnight I turned off the TV and wandered down to the kitchen to make myself a sandwich. I'd recently bought *The Elvis Cookbook* and had become obsessed with his favourite snack. It was a deep-fried peanut butter and banana sandwich. I made a couple of these and went down to sit by the river. In the moonlight I could see the bodies of the dead fish glistening in the water as they floated by. It was quite beautiful in a weird sort of way and I felt at peace for the first time in quite a while. London was all behind me, I loved our house and Ludmilla seemed happy. I was very excited about the new TV projects and even the fifty-foot chicken thing seemed less worrying after a couple of drinks. I was just finishing off the second sandwich when one of the dead fish started to move, its head flicking from side to side. It seemed to look straight at me and then, suddenly, started swimming towards me. I stared at it as it came right up to the bank and stuck its fat, decaying head out of the water. Then it spoke: 'What the fuck are you looking at, you fat prick.'

I looked behind me, wondering for a moment who the fish might be talking to. Then I realised that it was looking directly at me.

'Sorry, are you talking to me?' I asked the fish, trying to sound relaxed.

'See any other fat fuckers sitting around here?' replied the distinctly aggressive fish.

'Sorry, no, but I'm just not used to talking to fish – you

rather surprised me.' The fish made me really nervous.

'Listen, you fat fuck, I've been watching you and your dumb-ass bitch gormlessly wander round this place and you're getting on my fucking nerves. What the fuck are you doing with your life? What are you hiding away from down here?' The fish reminded me a bit of Arthur. I tried to look nonchalant again but failed miserably.

'Leave me alone. I just want to sit here and do nothing, stop hassling me. Why can't anything be normal? I move to the country and get fifty-foot chickens, talking dead fish and pig-dogs. I just want to be fucking normal.' I started crying, the tears flowing like mini waterfalls and pouring into the hot, sticky river in front of me. What was happening to me? I felt weak. I could see the fish staring at me and I felt incredibly hot. I could feel my heart racing faster and faster . . . was this it? Was this the end, a heart attack by a polluted river in front of an aggressive talking fish? I tried to stand up but felt dizzy. I thought I was going to be sick. I was getting panicky. I was sweating. I let go. Everything went black.

When I came to, it was dawn. The fish was gone and Ludmilla was shaking my shoulder, she looked really concerned. 'Goddamn it, JR, you gotta stop drinkin' and start acting like a real man. What the hell would your daddy say if he was alive?'

I was in quite a state. I prayed to whoever listened to this sort of stuff that if I was all right and survived all this I would change and be nicer to Ludmilla and try to get my shit together. I looked at her in the dawn light. She was still beautiful, but there were little worry lines at the sides of her eyes.

We walked back to the house together, arm in arm. She

made me a strong coffee and some toast as I sat at the kitchen table watching her. I had to get my shit together, start working again. I should let her do TV stuff, if that was what she enjoyed, stop being so selfish. I went up to bed and slept for nearly twenty-four hours. I woke up refreshed and ready to start again. It felt like a new dawn, something had changed. I wasn't going to take any other things in my life for granted, not fame, not friends, especially not Ludmilla.

Two weeks later she left me. I found out when a reporter from one of the Sunday tabloids rang me up to ask me how I felt about my wife spending the night in a hotel with Neil Morrissey. I was stupefied. I didn't know what he was talking about. She had been away for the night staying with her vegetable friend in the village setting up her display for the country fair. She didn't even know who Neil Morrissey was. He'd never been in *Dallas*, had he? The reporter was quite sweet really. Apparently Morrissey had been the celebrity brought in to open the fair and had been a guest judge at the vegetable competition. Clearly they had fallen for each other immediately. They had been photographed by the local newspaper snogging in the beer tent. The reporter said that they had checked into some swanky hotel about five miles from Chipping Bottom. I knew the one he meant – I had been intending to take her there as a surprise for her birthday. She came round with Morrissey three days later. He stayed outside in the car while she packed her stuff. I stood in the room watching her, trying to suppress my panic, trying to tell myself that it didn't matter. I would have more fun on my own, no restrictions, no one to answer to. I could fuck around again like in the good old days. I started crying again, it was becoming a bit of a habit. I pleaded with her not to leave but her face was blank; there was a strength to her that I'd never seen before. She'd moved on, I could see it.

'Ahoy, JR,' she whispered in my ear before kissing me softly on the cheek. She picked up her fake Louis Vuitton suitcase and walked off down the drive, tottering on her ludicrously high heels, her bum wiggling in her tiny miniskirt. She climbed in beside Morrissey who gave me a hesitant wave before burning off down the lane in his green sports car. In twenty seconds the car was out of sight and I was alone with Bacon. He bit my ankle softly, not even drawing blood as though he knew that this wasn't really the time.

Someone from the village dropped off a copy of the Sunday newspaper for me the next morning. There it was, a big colour picture of them both together, canoodling in a marquee. Inside the paper were more photos of them laughing together at what looked like a breakfast table and in a pub beer garden. She'd even consented to an interview. God knows how they'd done that, must have got some interpreter in. There it was in its full glory. The headline screamed: HELLO, WHAT? NO, I'M AN INSANE WASHED-UP MANIAC, NO, I'M RUBBISH. CIAO! All over a big picture of me shouting into a big mobile phone. The theme of the story was flop in the sack husband moved to the country only to suffer what Ludmilla called a shattering nervous breakdown. She said that I had claimed to have seen fifty-foot chickens and talked to fish and that I was drinking again and all the locals knew what I was like and hated me and that she could do no more for me. It was up to me now to save myself and she was doing all this in the hope that it would be a wake-up call to me to sort my life out. She also admitted to getting £200,000 for the story. She said that she'd been to a doctor who said that she had extraordinarily high levels of mercury in her blood and she felt that this came from the river near our house. She was sure that this was part of the reason that I had gone bananas. On page seven she was photographed topless sucking a banana.

I sat there for hours trying to sort out the stuff in my head. I couldn't really function any more, couldn't figure out what was real and what wasn't. Maybe the river was doing my head in? Maybe I had imagined the fish and the chickens? But what about the pub? What about Bacon? I started crying again. How had I got here, to this situation? I wasn't a bad man, I didn't deserve this. Or maybe I did? I thought about everyone I knew reading the paper and laughing to themselves. Schadenfreude, such a great German word for such a very British trait. Everyone would be very sympathetic but deep down would be loving the drama and their bit parts in it. Knowing glances in the street, a nudge to each other and pointing at you as though you were unable to see them. Cod-psychology journalists discussing what you should do next on some inane phone-in where every moron who could manage to dial a telephone number becomes a valid contributor. I couldn't face it all.

I opened the kitchen drawer and saw the racks of new Sabatier kitchen knives that Ludmilla had just purchased online from Czech Amazon for double the amount that it would have cost in the village shop. I ran my finger along the razor-sharp blade of the largest one. The skin cracked and the blood ran down the blade, dripping on to the kitchen counter. I could hear the ticking of the kitchen clock, louder and louder. Bacon barked in the garden, a car roared past the house, and then silence. The phone rang.

Epiphany

THAT PHONE CALL saved my life. It was ironic really. My
mobile phone was probably what I was best known for
and it was what had got me into this shit in the first place.
Maybe it was feeling guilty about it all? Whatever, it decided
to ring at the right time. It was my agent. He sounded very
excited.

Agent: Hey, Dom, sorry about Ludmilla. What are you
up to right now?
Me: I'm holding a large carving knife and I'm about
to kill myself.
Agent: Very funny, listen, you've got to get up to
London, the phones are going crazy, you're hot prop-
erty and we need to act as soon as possible.
Me: I'm not joking, I'm about to top myself, I'm really
depressed.
Agent: And I'm not joking – you're a walking ATM
machine at the moment. Get your arse up here right
now, I've sent a car down to Yokelville to pick you up.
Me: Seriously, I'm in a bad way.
Agent: Great, keep it all in your head for the book.
Me: What book?
Agent: Only the book that I've just negotiated for you
to write about your life.

Me: Oh.

Agent: What do you mean, oh! Three months ago we couldn't get a three grand advance for Hephalumps, that kids' book idea, now they're queuing up to read your story. Don't kick a gift horse in the mouth.

Me: It was Hephajumps, they can jump really high. That's their secret power. They're Hephajumpers.

Agent: Whatever, you're in business, have a shit and a shave, pack up and get your notorious arse up to London. We've got green lights on the reality projects as well. Let's make some money!

Me: OK, but I really don't feel tip-top.

I was on autopilot. I got changed and packed a small suitcase. I went outside and sat on a bench by the river and smoked fags until the car arrived. As we burned off down the lane I didn't look back at the house. I knew that I was never going back. I tried to find Bacon before I went but there was no sign of him. I guessed that he was probably better off in the wild. He'd never actually been that domesticated. I was starting to wonder whether he'd ever even existed. The talking fish and the tall chickens and the pig-dog seemed to be blurring into one. I really wanted a drink, but the car just had a copy of the Sunday newspaper with the picture of Ludmilla topless with the banana. She didn't even like bananas. That was thoughtful of the driver. Maybe there had been a line that I hadn't read? I opened the window and threw the whole newspaper out on to the road. The driver looked at me in the mirror but didn't say anything. I stared out of the window vacantly as we roared down the M40 towards London.

An hour or so later I was sitting in my agent's plush office in the most expensive part of Notting Hill Gate. He was in a top mood. He gave me an enormous pile of faxes and emails all with requests and offers on them.

Agent: Take a look at those, you are hot, hotter than hot, you're fucking scalding.

Me: Turn on the Xmas lights in Swindon, light the first firework at the Royal Agricultural College Bonfire Night, they're hardly offers of a cameo in the next Tarantino movie, are they?

Agent: Fucking hell, what the fuck do you want? We could clear half a mill if you agreed to all of these. Plus there's the book deal and we've got a meeting with Channel Five tomorrow about *Stuck in a Lift With You*. They're fucking mad for it, and they want you to be in the first one.

Me: I'm not being stuck in a fucking lift for three months, I just wanted to pitch the fucking thing.

Agent: They're paying top dollar, you'll be kept in the public eye for the whole time and it'll give you time to think about your book and get your head together.

Me: What, get my head together, while I'm sharing a fucking lift with James Hewitt?

Agent: It's definitely not Hewitt, they asked him, but he's playing Prince Charles in some TV movie about Diana.

Me: Whatever, it can't be any worse than the shit I'm living now. Let's do the meeting and then see what happens. Is that all for now? I need to go and get completely pissed. I'll see you tomorrow.

Agent: Yeah, go out and get it all out of your system.
Why don't you get yourself properly laid?
Me: Yeah maybe, let's see what happens. My wife only
technically left me this morning.

I left his office in a state of confusion. This was nothing
new. I liked my agent and he'd been great to me since we'd
met over the weatherman business but I always got the
impression that I was very low down on his order of importance. It was probably paranoia but I got the feeling that
he loathed me. Actually it probably wasn't paranoia.

I wasn't really in a fit state to go out but I did. I took a
cab into Soho. I hate the West End, especially at night. I
thought of Scorsese's *Taxi Driver*: 'One day a real rain's
gonna come, wash the scum off the streets.' I headed straight
for my club. I'd never been too sure why I'd joined a private
members' club. The idea of having a club was so archaic
and olde England it was everything that I loathed. On the
other hand it was always something a bit unachievable as
you needed to 'be someone' to become a member. I suppose
when membership was offered it felt like a recognition that
I had done something and so I accepted and then hung out
there for a couple of weeks until I realised that I loathed it.
I did use it occasionally when I had to meet someone in
central London. It was easier than sitting in a pub with
everyone setting their mobile phones to the horrible Nokia
ring and then setting them off whilst shouting 'HELLO, I'M
IN THE PUB.' At least in the club everyone was trying to
be way too cool to stare at anyone else. That would be an
admission that they were less important than the person
they were staring at and that was a definite no-no. My club,

a media one, was set up as a reaction to the stuffy old establishment clubs of Mayfair and St James's which didn't really cater for the cocaine-snorting new media elite. This, however, had been twenty years ago and so many new clubs had now been set up that my one felt like an old dinosaur, and had started to adopt the same stupid rules as the arcane ones it had sought to be an antidote to. I sat in the main bar and had an unbelievably expensive Mojito whilst trying to take in all the shit that had happened in the last couple of days. As the Mojito started to take its effect the doors of the bar opened and in staggered Morrissey and Ludmilla. They were pissed as newts and went straight up to the bar and ordered a bottle of champagne. Everyone present visibly tensed with anticipation, well aware of the first-class bit of gossip that had just materialised in front of them. I was tempted to do something but didn't have the energy. I got up and walked out, trying to retain as much dignity as possible. This didn't last too long. I went straight over to the sex shop about four hundred yards away and bought myself a bottle of poppers, or Amyl Nitrate as it was better known. For some reason this drug had always been legally sold and it was what we would buy when coming up to London from school for a cheap high. It was loathsome stuff and was rumoured to permanently kill off about a thousand brain cells a sniff, but I didn't care. The rush you got was intense and fleeting, your heart beating like an express train as the blood coursed round your body. It only lasted about a minute and then you were off again; it was the lowest of the low. I used an old trick and dipped a cigarette into the bottle before inhaling on the unlit fag. It was meltdown. I sat there for an hour or so, alone in Soho Square, off my tits on a drug that gay men used to loosen their sphincters. Eventually I hurled the glass bottle at a wall, got up, hailed a cab and checked myself into The Portobello Hotel in Notting Hill Gate. I slept like a baby.

I woke up the next day strangely euphoric. I had a bath in the same one that Johnny Depp had reputedly filled with champagne for Kate Moss only for a cleaning lady to empty it, mistaking the bubbly for dirty water. I got changed and took a cab to my agent's office. More requests had come in including an offer to star in a TV adaptation of *Three Men in a Boat* with Ainsley Harriot and Dale Winton. I had a cup of coffee with my agent before we set off for the meeting with Channel Five.

It all went swimmingly. They were really up for the idea of *Stuck in a Lift With You*. They had negotiated with Harvey Nichols the right to use one of their lifts for a year and they planned to do four shows, three months each. The two contestants would be given a weekly list of what was available in the food hall and ten pounds each to spend. The package would be lowered in through the little hatch at the top of the lift every Sunday evening. The show would have a regular slot three nights a week plus live web-cam feeds. They wanted to film mine first but not actually put it out live so that they could sort out teething problems. My show would go out, as live, at the end of the run. We struck a deal that I was very happy with and it was agreed that filming would start in three days. I asked who was going to share the lift with me but they were keen to keep it a secret as they felt it would be 'more fun' that way. I didn't really share their enthusiasm but as long as it wasn't James Hewitt, then I couldn't really care less. The bonus was that they'd signed up Oaksey to be the programme shrink. He'd been doing more and more of that kind of stuff and he's pretty good on telly. At least I knew that he'd be cool about me and I had the feeling that I needed a couple of one-on-ones so that would be useful.

We left the meeting and went on to a working lunch with the book people. They were keen for a 'warts and all' auto-biography and we agreed an advance and a rough deadline. I had checked with Channel Five and they were happy for me to take in paper and pen as I figured that the lift was going to be the perfect place to write the thing.

Three days later I was in a lift in Harvey Nichols waiting for the doors to open for the final time in three months to reveal whom I would be sharing the three square yards with. I heard a commotion outside, the sound of a couple of people applauding something and then the doors opened. In walked Vanessa Feltz.

The whole experience was quite traumatic. Vanessa turned out to be a lovely woman and, due to her recent marriage break-up and subsequent weight loss, did not take up as much room as you would have thought. We were suspicious of each other for the first week or so but our defences soon broke down and we actually developed a strong friendship. The days were long, hot and boring. The production team turned off the air-conditioning after the third day as they thought we were having too easy a time of it. Vanessa and I spent the rest of our time in the lift in our underwear, something which didn't do much for the ratings but which helped us survive the experience. I spent a lot of the time writing the book. Vanessa helped with spelling and gave really positive feedback on early drafts. It all came flowing out pretty easily and I'd finished the first draft by the time we were eventually released. Vanessa and I also came up with quite a catchy little tune that we called 'Stuck in a Lift With You' for obvious reasons. When we got out there was a lot of record company interest and we have recorded it and it should be out soon, maybe even this Christmas. I was able to have an hour a week in private with Oaksey while Vanessa listened to music on headphones. It was the best lot of sessions that I ever had with him. Being in there, stripped down to my pants and the bare essentials really made me do some tough thinking about life. A fan sent me a book on Bhuddism to read while I was in the lift. It was the only book that I had in there and I read it so many times that it fell apart. I have now converted to Bhuddism and it has really helped me to balance stuff in my life. I sold The Merkins to Gerald who has opened it up for Japanese tour groups as a bed and breakfast. He reckoned that no one would ever stay there long enough to really be affected by the river. It seems to be working really well. The Angry Peasant is now a sushi bar and Antony Worrall Thompson has bought the village shop and turned it into an organic deli. He apparently gets his produce from Badgergas Farm. I've bought another house, miles from the nearest river but still in the Cotswolds. Ludmilla split up with Neil Morrissey and is now the new gardening guru on *Ground Force*. Her life really has become *Being There*. I hope that she's happy. I think that I'm almost happy now. A woman who started up a *Trigger Happy* fan club kept pestering me to attend some convention where everyone had to dress as squirrels. I kept putting it off but finally relented. She looked after me and we really hit it off. In fact, we're married now and I've got a kid on the way. She is in no way judgemental. In fact she is still quite star-struck, which is great and the whole thing seems to work very well.

I've been holed away down here finishing the book and getting ready to do publicity for when *Stuck in a Lift* comes out. I'm a little worried as the whole publicity juggernaut revs itself up but I hope to roll with the punches. The BBC have even approached me to do another hidden camera type show. I think I'm almost ready for something like that now. I'm thinking of calling it *World Shut Your Mouth*. I haven't seen Arthur for nearly a year. I don't miss him.

So here's my story and this is my book. I hope that you enjoyed it. It's been weird looking back on everything. It all seems like a long bizarre dream. It's almost like none of this actually happened to me. Oscar Wilde said, 'Life is much too important a thing to talk seriously about.' I think he might have had a point.

ACKNOWLEDGEMENTS

THANKS VERY MUCH to Rosemary, Mary and everyone at Bloomsbury for being so nice, to Jo and Peter at PBJ for coping with me and to Alex Jackson-Long – I told you I'd do it.

Index

A NOTE ON THE AUTHOR

Dom Joly is an award-winning comedian and columnist. He lives unhappily with his partner André and their dog, Nigel, in Turkmenistan.

A NOTE ON THE TYPE

The text of this book is set in Linotype Sabon, named after the type founder, Jacques Sabon. It was designed by Jan Tschichold and jointly developed by Linotype, Monotype, and Stempel, in response to a need for a typeface to be available in identical form for mechanical hot metal composition and hand composition using foundry type. Tschichold based his design for Sabon roman on a font engraved by Garamond, and Sabon italic on a font by Granjon. It was first used in 1966 and has proved an enduring modern classic.

'If you thought TRIGGER HAPPY TV was well-observed, you'll discover it merely scratched the surface' HEAT

THE NO HOLDS BARRED AUTOBIOGRAPHY OF A MAN WITH THE EGO OF NAPOLEON AND THE TALENT OF DARREN DAY

This is the autobiography to end all autobiographies. Even as a baby, Dom Joly was like no other - he was born with a full head of hair and a complete set of teeth. As this memoir shows, the rest of his extraordinary life is filled with wild ups and downs, starting with his early years in the Lebanon with his first friend Arthur (a large Rhodesian Ridgeback). We follow Joly through a two-year prison sentence in Tangiers, student insurrection at a London poly, espionage, a flirtation with British politics and a low-life stint in Notting Hill. Then Joly gets his lucky break while attending the Priory, leading to celebville, a country pile called The Merkins, Vanessa Feltz and TRIGGER HAPPY TV. And every word is completely, unadulteratedly and unarguably true...

'Joly serves up a narrative of the bizarre and improbable ... Brutal electrocution of a nanny, a fling with Nigel from Turkmenistan and a stint at MI6 rouse laughs aplenty' OBSERVER

'It's the kind of book that can genuinely make you laugh out loud and cause people sitting next to you to move slightly further away ... Joly is on outstanding form throughout, and creates some fantastic set-pieces ... an essential read' EXPOSÉ

'Joly is a very funny man indeed ... his style is particularly winning – both bouncy and lyrical ... This really is a super read!' STAR MAGAZINE

ISBN 0-7475-7760-9

bloomsbury pbks

£7.99
www.bloomsbury.com

9 780747 577607

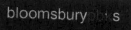